At home with Flowers

At home with Flowers

Compiled by Coral Walker

LONGMEADOW
P R E S S

A SALAMANDER BOOK

Copyright © 1993 by Salamander Books Ltd.,
129-137 York Way, London N7 9LG,
United Kingdom.

Published by Longmeadow Press,
201 High Ridge Road, Stamford, CT 16904

Designed and edited by Brown Packaging Ltd.,
255-257 Liverpool Road, London N1 1LX.

Cover & Interior Design by: Kathy Gummer

ISBN 0-681-45468-7

Printed in Italy

First Longmeadow Press Edition

9 8 7 6 5 4 3 2 1

This book may not be sold outside the United
States of America or Canada.

A NOTE TO READERS

The publishers would like to advise you that
some flowers featured in this book may cause
an allergic response in a very limited number
of individuals. In the unlikely event of this
happening, we suggest you consult a doctor.

CREDITS
Flower Designs by: Jan Hall,
Mary Lawrence, Jane Newdick, Judy Taylor
and Sarah Waterkeyn

Consultants: Mary Lawrence, David Squire

Photographers: Di Lewis, Richard Paines,
Helen Pask and Steve Tanner

Managing Editor: Jilly Glassborow

Color Separation by:
Scantrans Pte Ltd., Singapore.

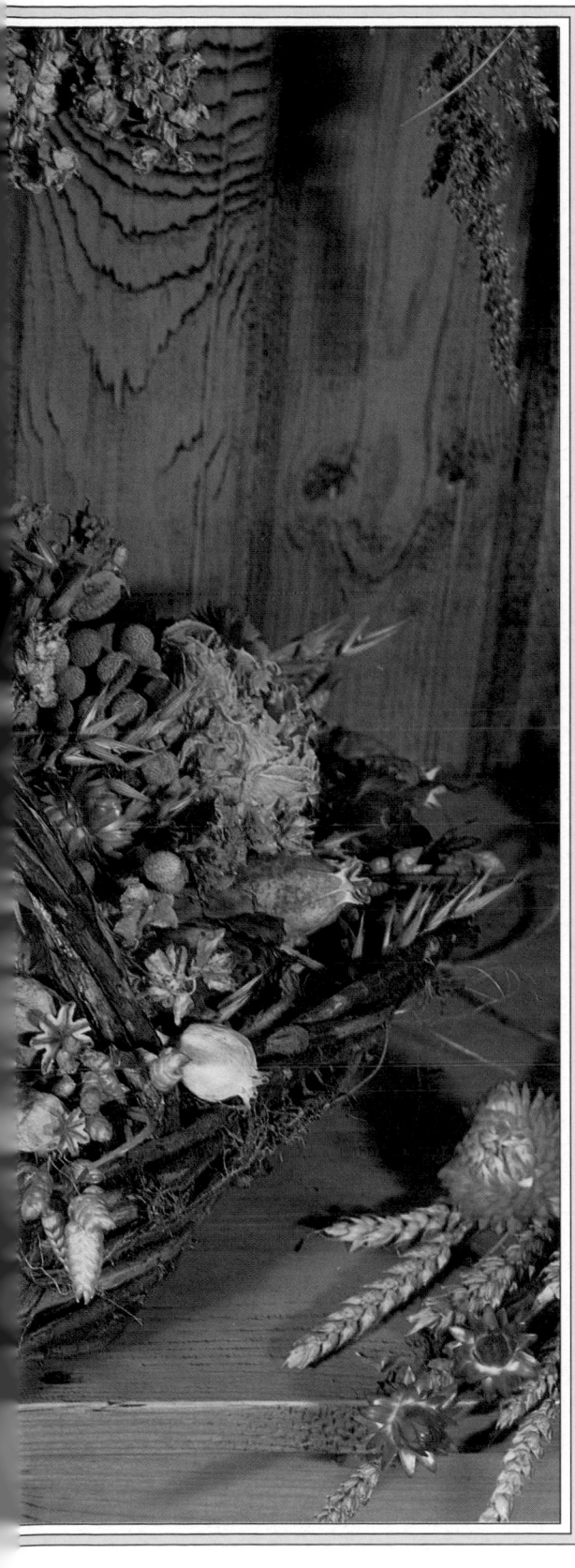

CONTENTS

$\mathscr{I}$NTRODUCTION

Over the years, much has been written about the beauty of flowers and the pleasure they bring. Anyone interested in growing, displaying or preserving flowers will already know just how satisfying it is to work with them, and how they can enhance every home and almost every occasion.

$\mathscr{A}$t Home With Flowers has been compiled as a comprehensive, informative and inspirational tool for the flower lover, whether a seasoned old-timer or someone new to the delights of all things floral. It endeavours to explore the versatility of flowers: to capture their fast-fading beauty and make the very best of all their properties.

In each chapter there is a wide variety of colourfully illustrated projects, which have simple explanations, and there are also full instructions on any techniques, materials and equipment you might need.

Fresh flowers are presented in a wide variety of ways, with designs that can be copied or used to gain inspiration. There is also a full guide to conditioning and caring for different flower types on pages 148-151 which will enable you to keep fresh blooms as long as possible.

There are three chapters devoted to preserved flowers — dried, pressed and pot-pourri — plus full information on preservation methods and fabulous decorations, recipes, designs and gifts you can make.

Flowers for Beauty uses the healing and medicinal properties of plants in a number of easy-to-follow recipes for making your own beauty preparations, while the exotic and edible qualities of many flowers are explored in *Flowers as Food*.

Once you've tried your hand at some of these techniques and ideas, you might want to use them to give as presents. *Floral Gifts* has a large selection of floral presents to make for everyone.

Finally, we list popular flowers to grow in an easy-to-follow chart and give a guide to their best use. In most cases throughout the book, the plants are referred to by their common names with alternative American names given in brackets where necessary. However, a full list on page 166 gives both the common name in addition to the botanical name for easy reference.

Like flowers themselves, there is something in *At Home With Flowers* to please everyone. Whether it is used occasionally or often it makes wonderful browsing and helps to demonstrate that, indeed, the beauty of flowers and the joy they can bring, transcends fads, fashion and time.

A frosted glass vase in pale mauve is the perfect foil for fresh lavender. Later you can use the flowerheads for pot-pourri.

EXOTIC MEDLEY

Orange lilies
Pink 'Stargazer' lilies
Pink larkspur
Nasturtiums
Bright pink pelargoniums
Pale yellow and mid pink alstroemeria
Garden marigolds
Onion heads
Pink roses
African daisies
Deep magenta carnations
Selection of jugs

The inspiration for this exotic fantasy is a richly patterned tablecloth with leaves, flowers and birds. A group of vases filled with vivid blooms such as these would make a perfect decoration for an evening buffet or garden party.

The flowers are very simply arranged, relying on the fusion of bright, clashing colours and strong contours.

Here, the strong orange in the tablecloth has been picked as the basic colour for the display, and orange lilies make a bold start in the larger green jug. Mix them with several pink lilies, a couple of pink roses and place a few long stems of larkspur to the back of the jug.

The round, pink vase contains a handful or two of orange nasturtiums, shocking-pink pelargoniums and pinkish alstroemeria. The neighbouring vase has a mixture of alstroemeria, marigolds and some more of the orange lilies.

The smaller of the two green jugs holds most of the lily blooms, this time combined with onion heads, roses, pelargoniums, carnations and daisies.

This Exotic Medley of rich colours takes its inspiration from the boldly patterned table cover. The result is almost tropical.

ABOVE: Rich red ranunculus and pale green bells of Ireland provide a soft, velvet texture.

RED VELVET

Bells of Ireland
Garlic flowerheads
White statice
Summer cypress (Kochia scoparia)
Pink scabious (pincushion flowers)
Red ranunculus
Laurustinus
Water jug and bowl
Florists' foam

An old water jug and bowl provide the perfect setting for this traditional arrangement, with its bold colours and contours.

Wedge left-over scraps of soaked foam into the jug. Then position a few large stems of bells of Ireland with two or three garlic flowerheads to establish the height and outline. Fill in the outline with the summer cypress and statice, keeping the stems at least 2in (5cm) shorter than the garlic and bells of Ireland. Then add the scabious throughout the display.

Brilliant red ranunculus instantly lift the arrangement, their colour and texture a striking contrast to the existing plants. To finish the display, tuck in a few stems of flowering laurustinus.

Laurustinus
Eucalyptus
Red spray carnations and buds
Shiny kitchen bakeware
Florists' foam
Silver paint spray

The kitchen is often the first place to look for useful and attractive containers. Pretty aluminium cases, such as the ones that have been used in this arrangement, are shiny and create attractive highlights.

First, spray some longer stems of eucalyptus with silver spray paint. Make sure that you do this in a well-ventilated room — paint fumes can be quite toxic if they are inhaled. Leave the eucalyptus to dry on a piece of newspaper. It will not take long, and in the meantime you can begin building up the display.

Place a piece of soaked florists' foam in the baking case, then create the outline of the arrangement with some long stems of laurustinus. Once the eucalyptus is dry, slot it in among the laurustinus.

Use the carnations to form the focal point of the display and fill in any gaps with carnation buds and flowers. Finally, for depth, recess some dark red laurustinus buds.

HARVEST GARLAND

Ripe ears of wheat
Field poppies (fresh or artificial), or
common marigolds
Chamomile flowers
Cornflowers
Florists' foam ring
Florists' wire

Harvest festival garlands are so often made from dried flowers, so this fresh one makes a delightful change. However, fresh poppies do not last very long so you may

ABOVE: This Harvest Garland has been made from ripe ears of wheat, poppies, cornflowers and chamomile.

choose to use artificial ones instead.

Soak the foam ring well and build up the garland with the wheat, ensuring that the ears follow the same direction. Tuck in the cornflowers fairly evenly around the garland and add the chamomile flowers. Finish with the bright red poppies or, for a longer lasting display, you can use common or pot marigolds instead.

ABOVE: These bright and shiny baking tins make great containers for silver-sprayed foliage and bright blooms.

 14

SCARLET ANEMONES

Red anemones
Marguerite foliage
Small-headed asters (September flowers)
Colander or round bowl
Saucer
Florists' foam
Florists' tape
Florists' putty

Brilliant scarlet anemones dominate this lovely arrangement, which nestles in an old-fashioned enamelled colander. You could use any round bowl or dish.

First, tape a piece of soaked florists' foam to a saucer and secure it inside the colander with a little putty.

Cover the foam with feathery marguerite foliage and form the dome-shaped outline for the other flowers. Follow this rounded

ABOVE: Create a cheerful display with brilliant red anemones and tiny asters.

design with the anemones, positioning them so that their faces look up and out.

Offset the deep reds and greens of the anemones and the marguerite foliage with sprays of asters, tucking them in throughout the arrangement.

 15

LILY BOUQUET

Lilies (Lilium longiflorum)
Snowball flowers (Viburnum opulus)
Iris or gladioli leaves
Florists' wire

The strong, uncluttered shape and heady fragrance of *Lilium longiflorum* makes it an ideal flower for a wedding bouquet.

This bouquet is a simple sheaf and is very easily constructed. It is designed to be carried resting over one arm, with the stems supported by the opposite hand.

Begin by stripping the lower leaves from the stems of the snowball flowers. You can strengthen the heavy flowerheads by using a fine silver wire.

Then take the first lily in one hand to determine the length of the bouquet. With the other hand begin to build up the bouquet, gathering the lilies and snowball flowers and placing them so that the heads graduate down toward the handhold.

When you are happy with the shape, bind wire firmly around the stems, just under the lowest flowerheads, and trim the stems to the same length. Cover the wire with long, narrow iris or gladioli leaves.

OPEN BOX

Common or English laurel
Yellow double tulips
Cream spider chrysanthemums
Cream coloured lilies
Wooden box
Twig
Plate
Florists' foam
Florists' tape

Bring out the warm sheen of a lovely wooden box by filling it with lustrous laurel leaves and creamy-yellow flowerheads.

LEFT: The large white trumpet lilies in this striking sheaf make a beautiful bouquet for the modern bride.

Tape soaked florists' foam to a plate before inserting it into the box. Now prop open the box lid with a small twig.

Create the outline of the arrangement with the laurel, covering the foam and filling the open box. Next, cut the tulips on the slant so that they slot into the foam more easily. Keep them the same length and position them throughout the display. Push in the spider chrysanthemums to add depth and contrast, and finish off with the focal flowers, the lilies.

YELLOW TRIO

Gerbera
Foliage
Yellow broom
Cocktail shaker
Florists' foam

ABOVE: A profusion of lilies, tulips and laurel tumble out of this old wooden box.

A cocktail shaker doubles up as a vase for this highly effective yet simple arrangement. Put a piece of soaked florists' foam into the shaker base, then insert three gerbera flowers, graduating the length of the stems. Add just a little foliage (in this case carnation foliage) behind and in front of the second tallest gerbera.

Position some curving sprays of yellow broom on either side of the display. The spiky flowers of the broom contrast with the soft petals of the gerbera.

Reserve some short stems of broom and insert these into a small piece of soaked florists' foam which has been postioned in the shaker lid. To complete the effect, place this at the base of the main arrangement.

BELOW: With only three main flowers, Yellow Trio proves how effective a simple design can be.

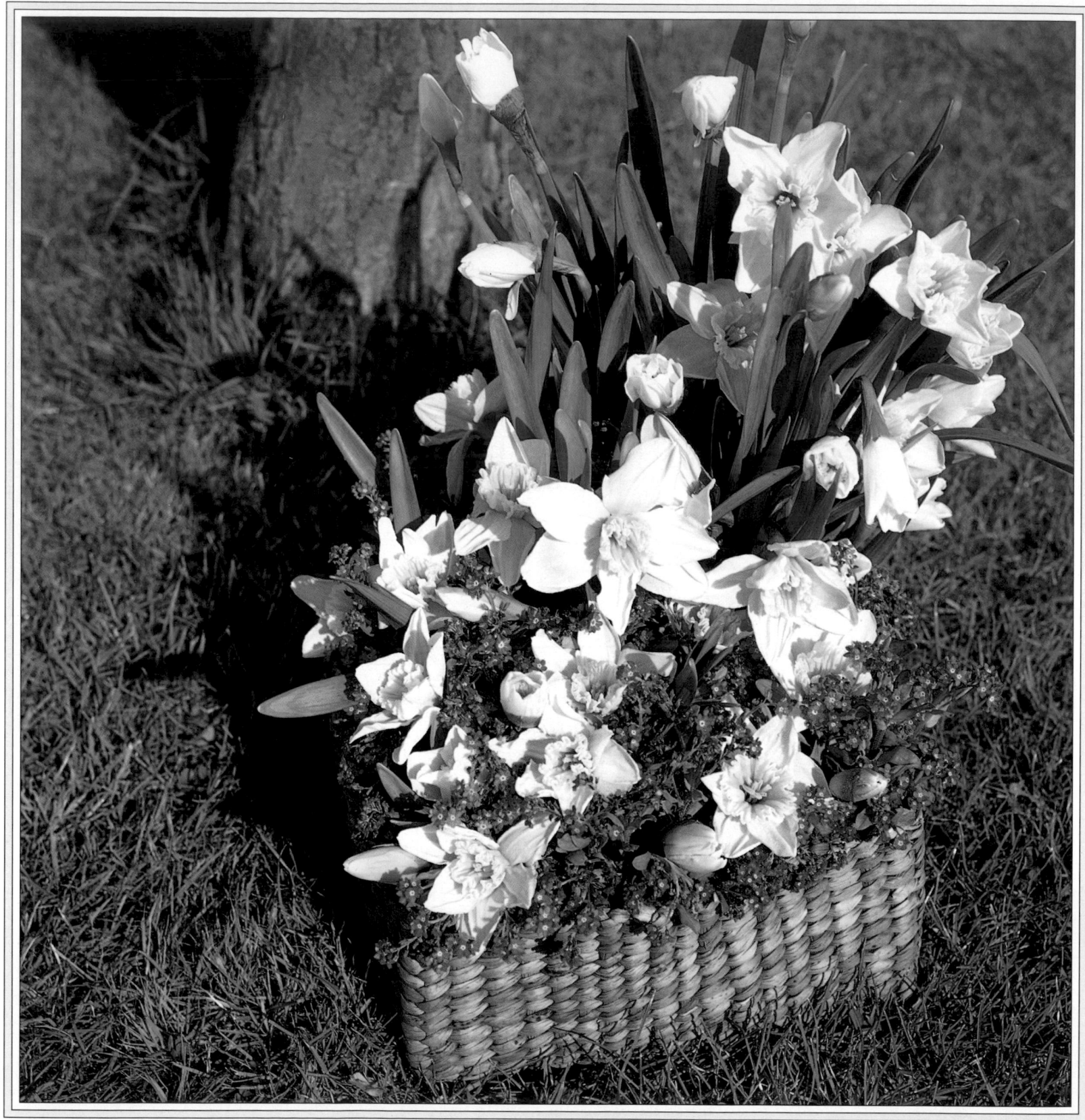

SPRING CHORUS

Daffodils and leaves
Forget-me-nots
Straw basket
Plastic container to fit inside basket
Wire mesh

A wicker basket provides a country setting for this charming display of spring daffodils and early forget-me-nots. Before starting your display, line the basket with a plastic container to protect it and fill this with crushed wire mesh.

Position a bunch of daffodils at the back of the container, adding daffodil leaves to give a natural look. Then group the forget-me-nots into several small bunches and insert them throughout the basket, tucking some into the front so that they just peep over the edge.

Finally, cut down the remaining daffodils and position these at random among the forget-me-not bunches to complete this picturesque country display.

SPRINGTIME POSY

White lilac
Blue hyacinths
Pale yellow roses
Yellow freesia
Paper doily
Rubber band or florists' wire twist
Glue
Ribbon (optional)

Posies are simple to put together, yet the finished results are so satisfying.

First, condition the lilac by standing the stripped short stems in 2in (5cm) of boiling water for two minutes, then give them a cool drink for several hours. Gather all the flowers into a bunch, trim the stems to the same length and then bind the posy with a florists' wire twist or rubber band.

Cut to the centre of the doily, and cut out enough of the centre to accommodate the flowers. Wrap the doily around the posy and overlap the edges, securing them with a little glue. Finish off with some ribbon.

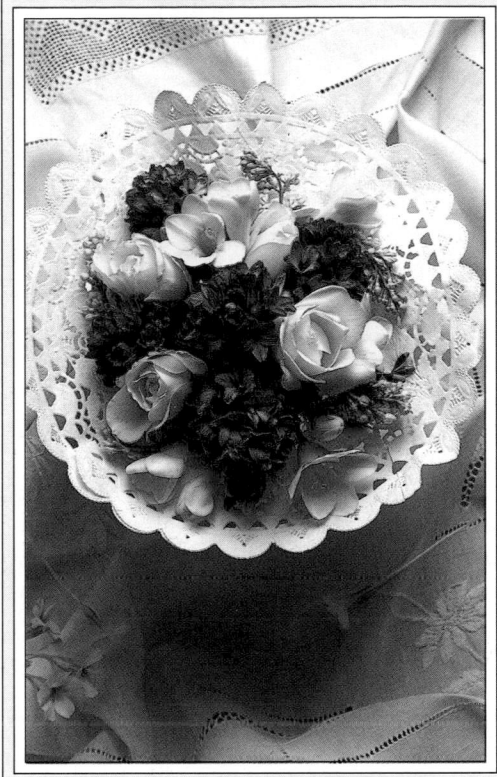

ABOVE: This attractive, scented posy, easily assembled, would be sure to delight any recipient.

AMETHYST ARRAY

Larkspur (Delphinium elatum)
Bouvardia
Alstroemeria
Traditional salt jar
Florists' foam

In this attractive arrangement, gently flowing lines and contours have been created with just three varieties of flowers. And the ceramic salt jar — with its 'open mouth' — provides the perfect backdrop.

First, wedge a piece of soaked foam into the mouth of the jar. Then form a gently curving horizontal line with the larkspur. Push a little bouvardia into the jar to provide some depth to the arrangement and finish off with the alstroemeria as the focal flowers, allowing a few longer stems to protrude and strengthen the outline.

LEFT: A country-style basket is packed with spring forget-me-nots and daffodils.

ABOVE: Amethyst-blue larkspur set the scene for clusters of alstroemeria.

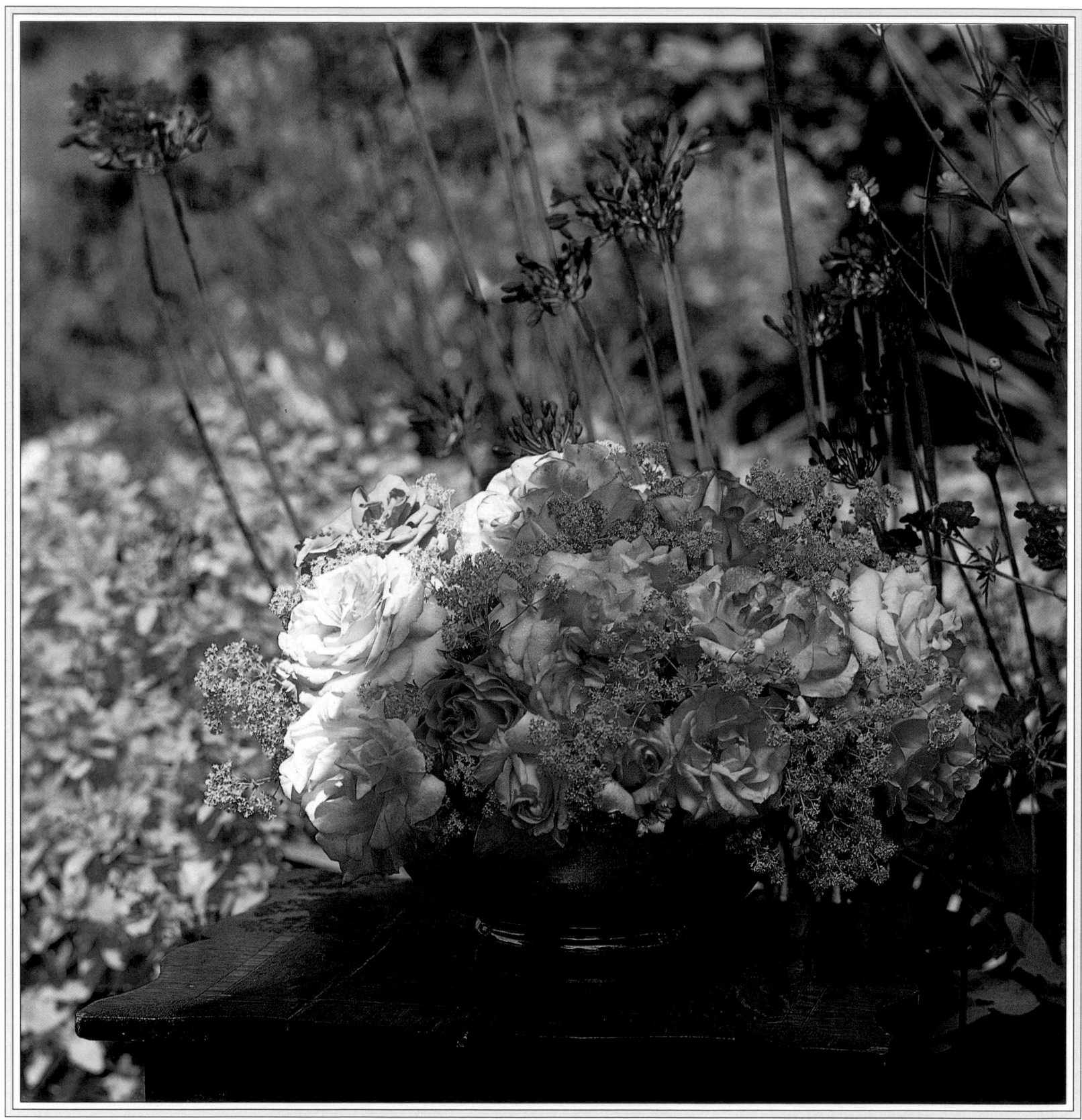

BUTTERY YELLOW

Yellow and apricot coloured roses
Lady's mantle
Shallow bowl
Wire mesh

Little can match the beauty of full-blown garden roses, and a pretty lustre bowl with a gilt base is ideal for this rich mix of buttery yellow and soft peach.

Crumple the wire mesh and push it into the bowl. Fill with water. Cut the stems of the roses quite short so that the flowers sit close to the bowl. Push each one into the mesh until you have an even dome shape.

Finally, tuck in some sprays of acid green lady's mantle to offset the roses and bring the whole display to life.

LEFT: A golden lustre bowl is filled with buttery yellow roses and green lady's mantle.

BELOW: Lofty delphiniums create a magnificent floor-standing display.

ABOVE: Put a redundant goldfish bowl to good use with this eye-catching arrangement.

DELPHINIUM BLUE

Delphiniums
Yellow antirrhinums
Blue/mauve hydrangeas
Large vase
Wire mesh
Florists' tape

Choose a tall, sturdy vase and bold, elegant flowers to create a stunning floor-standing arrangement which will complement any sitting room or hallway.

Loosely pack the vase with the crumpled wire mesh. Bend a circle of wire mesh to overlap the rim of the vase and secure it in place with florists' tape. Then fill the vase with water.

Place the tallest delphinium in the centre of the vase. Position the others in front and to the side of the central stem, graduating the flowers downward in height to create a well-balanced effect.

Intersperse the delphiniums with antirrhinums, following the line of the design. To complete, form a collar of hydrangea blooms around the neck of the vase.

SEASCAPE

Gypsophila (baby's breath)
Brodiaea
Peach spray carnations
Dried onion heads
Goldfish bowl
Seashells and pebbles

A goldfish bowl and seashells form the setting for this attractive and unusual free-flowing arrangement. First, fill the bowl carefully with a mixture of shells and pebbles before adding the water.

The aim is to achieve a 'waterspray' effect with the first few flowers. Start with gypsophila (baby's breath), trailing a little over the side. Next add stems of delicate blue *Brodiaea*, following the same outline.

Peach spray carnations reflect the colour in some of the seashells and only a few are needed to follow the sweeping outline that you have already established. Dried onion heads have a lovely texture and their colour is picked up by the pebbles and shells. Place eight or so throughout the arrangement, filling in the outline.

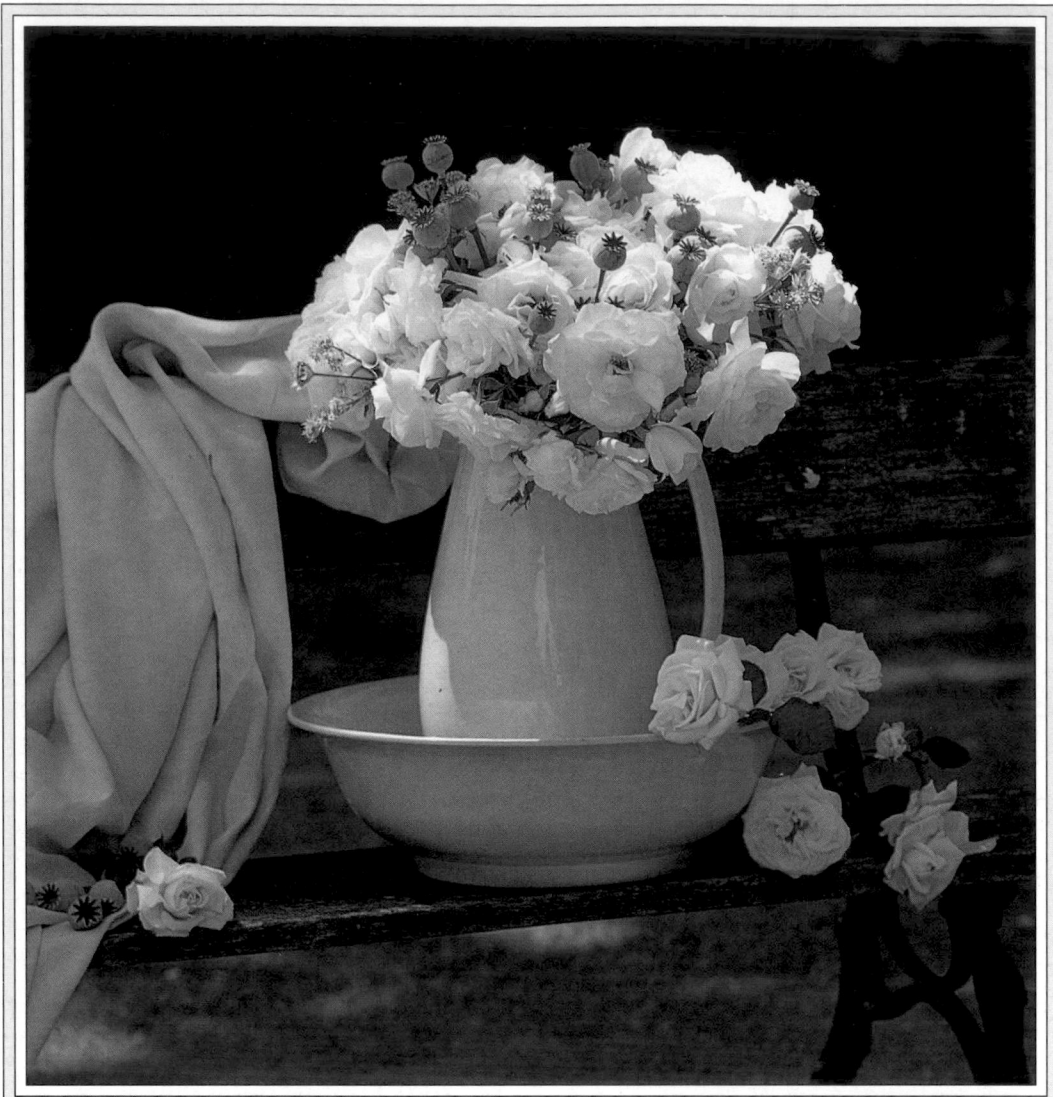

White 'Iceberg' roses
Poppy seedheads
White water jug and bowl

'Iceberg' roses have a freshness and simplicity that few blooms can match. They demand a simple treatment, too, to achieve the best effect.

First fill the jug with water and then add a good bunchful of the roses, keeping some

GARLAND IN WHITE

White gladioli
Chervil
Cow parsley (alternatively, meadow parsley or wild carrot)
White chrysanthemums
Rue
Variegated geranium foliage
Eucalyptus
Poppy and flax seedheads
Florists' foam ring

This lovely garland is made from shades of cream, green and white. It provides welcome relief from heavier, winter displays.

ABOVE: 'Iceberg' roses tumble from a graceful plain white jug and bowl and combine well with the aqua-silver of poppy seedheads.

Soak the foam ring well and begin making the garland by inserting the eucalyptus and other foliage in clusters. Next, add groups of chervil and cow parsley. Tuck in two or three chrysanthemum flowerheads and poppy and flax seedheads. Finally, work round the garland with the principal flowers — the gladioli.

Keep all the stems short and condition the rue and the wildflowers overnight before you use them.

of them upright, allowing others to nod gently over the edge of the jug. Intersperse the arrangement with poppy seedheads; you will find that their natural silvery blue hue makes the perfect match.

Finish off with a few roses resting in a little water in the bowl.

BELOW: White gladioli and chrysanthemums, combined with variegated foliage in shades of cream and green, create a serene effect.

ABOVE: Cool shades of green foliage and glass create a tranquil display.

TRANQUILLITY

Bear grass
Birds of paradise leaves
Bells of Ireland
Leucodendron foliage
Snow-on-the-mountain
Green glass jugs or tankards
Green marbles

This serene display uses only shades of green to achieve the tranquil effect.

To begin, place marbles in the bottom of the larger jug and half fill the jug with water. Then build up the basic outline with bear grass, allowing the blades to curve out on either side. Use birds of paradise leaves in the centre of the grass.

Add two stems of bells of Ireland next, one slightly shorter than the other, then fill out the display with *Leucodendron* foliage. Finish off the arrangement with a few pieces of variegated snow-on-the-mountain at the front.

The smaller jug holds only a clump of snow-on-the-mountain and, set as it is next to its larger counterpart, it completes the picture beautifully.

 25

ORIENTAL BLOSSOM

Sprays of apple blossom
Pink tulips
Chinese-style bowl
Large metal pinholder
Florists' foam

The natural simplicity and freshness of flowering apple blossom combined with pale pink tulips adds a timeless tranquillity to this Oriental setting. A Chinese bowl gives a touch of authenticity.

Use a large metal pinholder in the bottom of the bowl to act as a balance and fill the bowl with well-soaked florists' foam.

Strip the bark from the lower stems of the apple branches and crush them well with a hammer to aid water absorption.

Position two branches at the back of the bowl at an oblique angle. Place shorter branches at the front of the bowl at the same angle. Put one more branch at the front of the bowl, positioning it so that it bends down to touch the table.

Starting from the left, and following the line of the final branch, position the tulips to create a central focal point.

RIGHT: The lines of this minimalist display are taken from the Oriental style of flower arrangement.

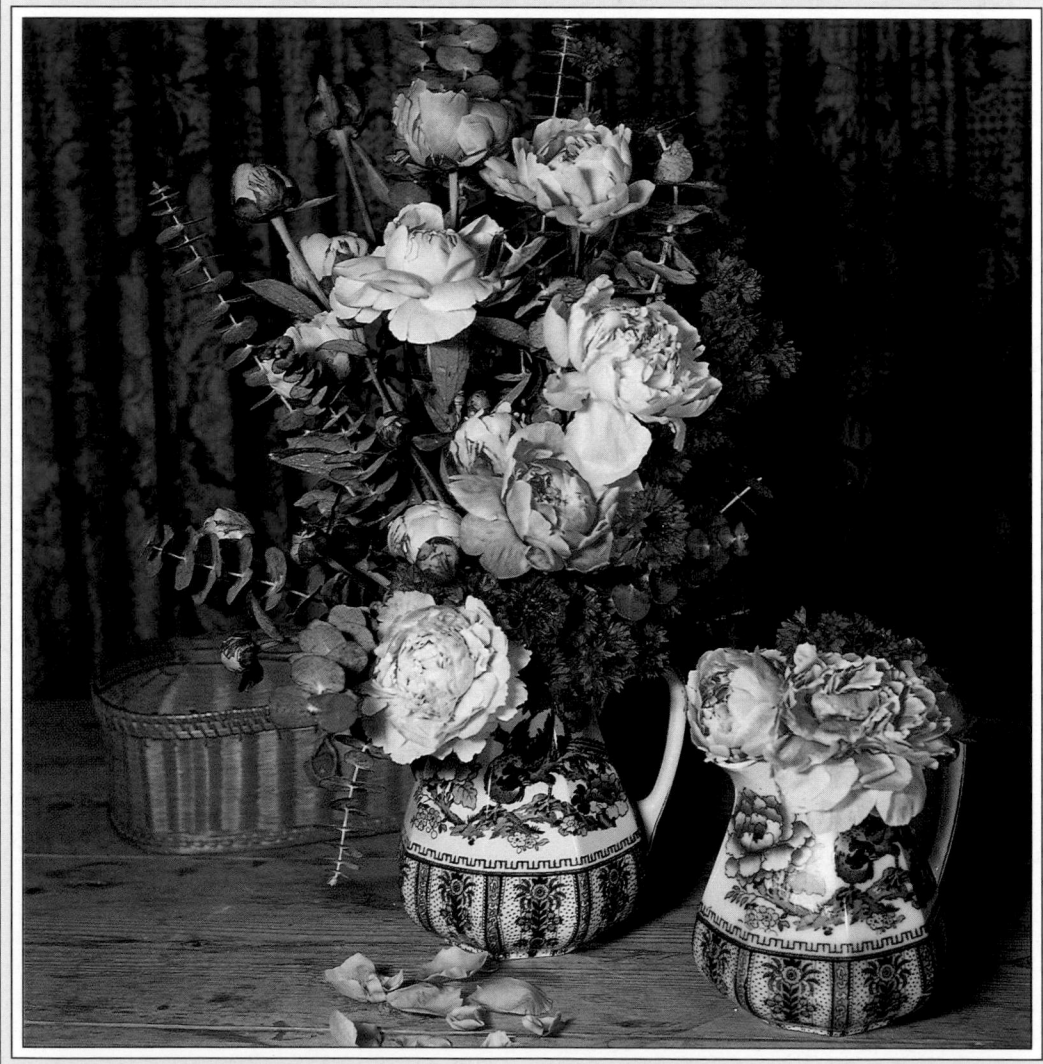

DUET FOR PEONIES

Pink peonies
Blue cornflowers
Eucalyptus foliage
Matching jugs
String

The floral design on these pretty blue and pink patterned jugs is beautifully complemented by the choice of peonies and cornflowers. You will need at least 20 peonies — both open and in bud — although it will depend upon the size of your jugs.

The main display in the larger of the two jugs is bunched and tied with string before it is put into the container. This slightly more unusual type of flower arrangement, often known as a hostess bunch, provides a good alternative to using florists' foam.

Arrange a fan shape of eucalyptus in one hand and secure this with string. Bind the peonies firmly into the bunch, following the shape of the eucalyptus and adding in extra budding peonies, open peonies and foliage as you work.

Next add a flourish of cornflowers down one side of the jug and finish the arrange-

LEFT: Multi-petalled peonies make wonderful, rich displays. These pretty pale pink peonies are offset by the deep blue of the cornflowers.

ment with a short bunch at the base of the display. Firmly secure the bunch with more string and insert it into the jug.

For the arrangement in the smaller jug, cut down some peonies so that the heads sit neatly into the rim of the jug. To finish off, position a few of the cornflowers in the centre of the display.

Make sure that you keep the water levels in the jugs topped up so that the flowers last for as long as possible.

BELOW: The bold, sunny faces of coral-pink gerbera form the focal point of this traditional display.

PINK GERBERA

Eucalyptus
Small-headed asters (September flowers)
Pink gladioli
White and blue delphiniums
Pink gerbera
White spray chrysanthemums
Bells of Ireland
Vase

Originally from South Africa, gerbera are now widely available internationally as cut flowers. Their bold flowerheads and wonderful array of colours make them the ideal focal point for any display.

Fill the vase with water and build up the outline using eucalyptus and some small-headed asters. (These little daisy-type flowers are often known as September flowers in Britain.) Curve the eucalyptus down toward the base of the display and position the feathery asters upright at the back.

Add to the outline by inserting a few short stems of gladioli, then fill in with white and blue delphiniums.

Now position the gerbera, keeping them to the foreground of the display and allowing one to drape over the front of the vase. Recess a few chrysanthemums and finish off with two or three stems of bells of Ireland for an interesting textural contrast.

ABOVE: The pink and peach blooms of roses and carnations nestle in a pretty glass bowl.

PINK AND PEACH ROSE BOWL

Pink/peach floribunda roses
Deep peach carnations
Paler peach carnations
Variegated ivy
Posy bowl
Florists' foam

Old-fashioned pink glass makes an ideal setting for this pleasing arrangement.

Fill the bowl with soaked florists' foam. Place the ivy leaves around the edge, overlapping them a little. To establish the height of the display, measure a single rosebud stem against the bowl — it should be the height of the container plus a third. Position this rose in the centre of the bowl and add the remaining roses, turning the bowl as you work to create an even effect.

Fill in with carnations, taking care not to overlap the ivy leaves. Tuck in a few more ivy leaves throughout the display.

ROSE BASKET

Selection of old-fashioned garden roses such as
'Baron Girod L'Ain', 'Celeste',
Rosa gallica 'Officinalis' or 'Fantin Latour'
Wicker basket with handle
Florists' foam
Polythene or plastic bag

Full-blown early summer roses capture the look of a Fantin-Latour painting. The many- petalled blooms are richly perfumed and softly coloured, and anything else with them would spoil their perfection.

Line the basket with polythene, and pack it with well-soaked florists' foam. Make sure the roses have been well conditioned and the lower leaves have been stripped off (see page 9). Then insert them into the basket, fairly randomly, making sure that the whole display is no higher than the handle.

RIGHT: A selection of old-fashioned roses in a rustic basket brings a wonderfully fragrant touch of the countryside into the home.

 28

SWEEPING FERN

Sprengeri fern (Asparagus sprengeri)
Creamy-pink alstroemeria
White lilac
Pink daisy chrysanthemums
Tall vase

A tall, curving vase sets the style for this elegant, sweeping arrangement. Put only water into the vase as the narrow neck will support the display.

Take a few long stems of fern, positioning some upright and curving one large piece so that it sweeps down in front of the vase. Then add two long stems and one shorter one of alstroemeria.

Create a central column by using white lilac; this will give depth to the display. Finally, take stems of chrysanthemums in graduating lengths and place them throughout the arrangement.

BELOW: Soft curving lines of feathery fern sweep down from a profusion of sugary-pink and cream blooms.

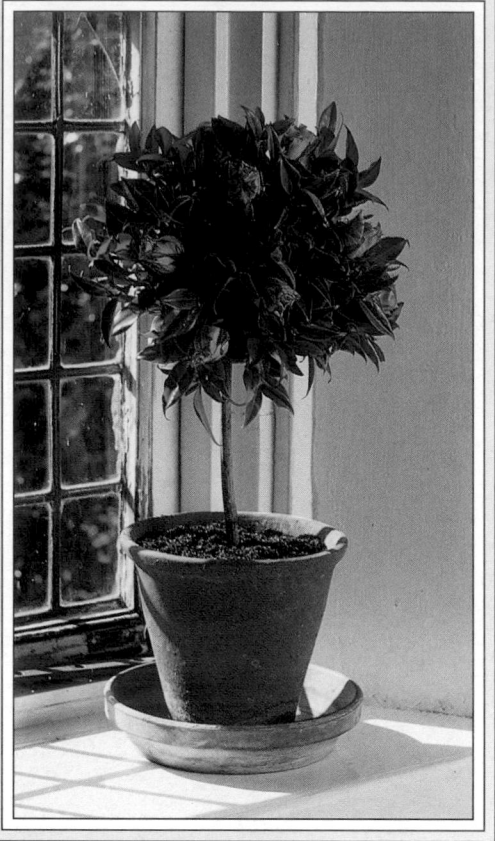

ABOVE: A miniature potted tree is easy to assemble from shiny leaves and rosebuds.

FRESH FLOWER TREE

Small evergreen leaves such as camellia tips,
laurustinus, or Mexican orange
Large rosebuds
Terracotta pot and saucer
Soil
Small straight branch
Florists' foam brick
Wet florists' foam sphere

Miniature trees made from leaves and flowers make charming displays, particularly if used in pairs.

Tightly pack an old terracotta pot with florists' foam and push in a straight stick or small branch. Wedge a well-soaked foam sphere on to the top of the stick.

Insert the foliage into the sphere, turning the pot as you work to keep an even shape.

Cut the stems of the roses fairly short — while necessary for this design, it will also enable the water to reach the flowerheads. Tuck the rosebuds in among the leaves and finish with some soil around the base to cover the foam.

The woody stems of the shrubs and roses will need to be well conditioned before inserting them into this display. This will ensure that the plants last as long as possible. (For conditioning tips, see page 9).

IVY SWAG WITH LILIES

Glossy ivy
White lilies (Lilium longiflorum
and Lilium 'Mont Blanc')
Artificial fruit or berries
Small tray
Reel wire
Florists' foam
Masking tape or drawing pins
Red cord

This stunning swag is made simply from trailing ivy. It is offset with a glorious display of white lilies, which are perfect for a special occasion.

Begin by forming the swag. Measure out a piece of red cord the length you wish the swag to be. Using reel wire, secure the ivy along the cord, joining short pieces of ivy together with more wire as necessary.

The swag can then be looped along a mantelpiece, above a doorway or across a piece of furniture such as a buffet table. Secure it with masking tape or pins. You can wire in pieces of artificial fruit for a more bountiful effect.

For the lily arrangement, tape a brick of soaked florists' foam to a tray. Trim and clean more of the glossy green ivy foliage and use it to cover the foam. Tuck in the smaller lilies and the lily buds. Use the *Lilium longiflorum* blooms to form the focal point of the display.

RIGHT: Loops of glossy green ivy contrast with pure white lilies.

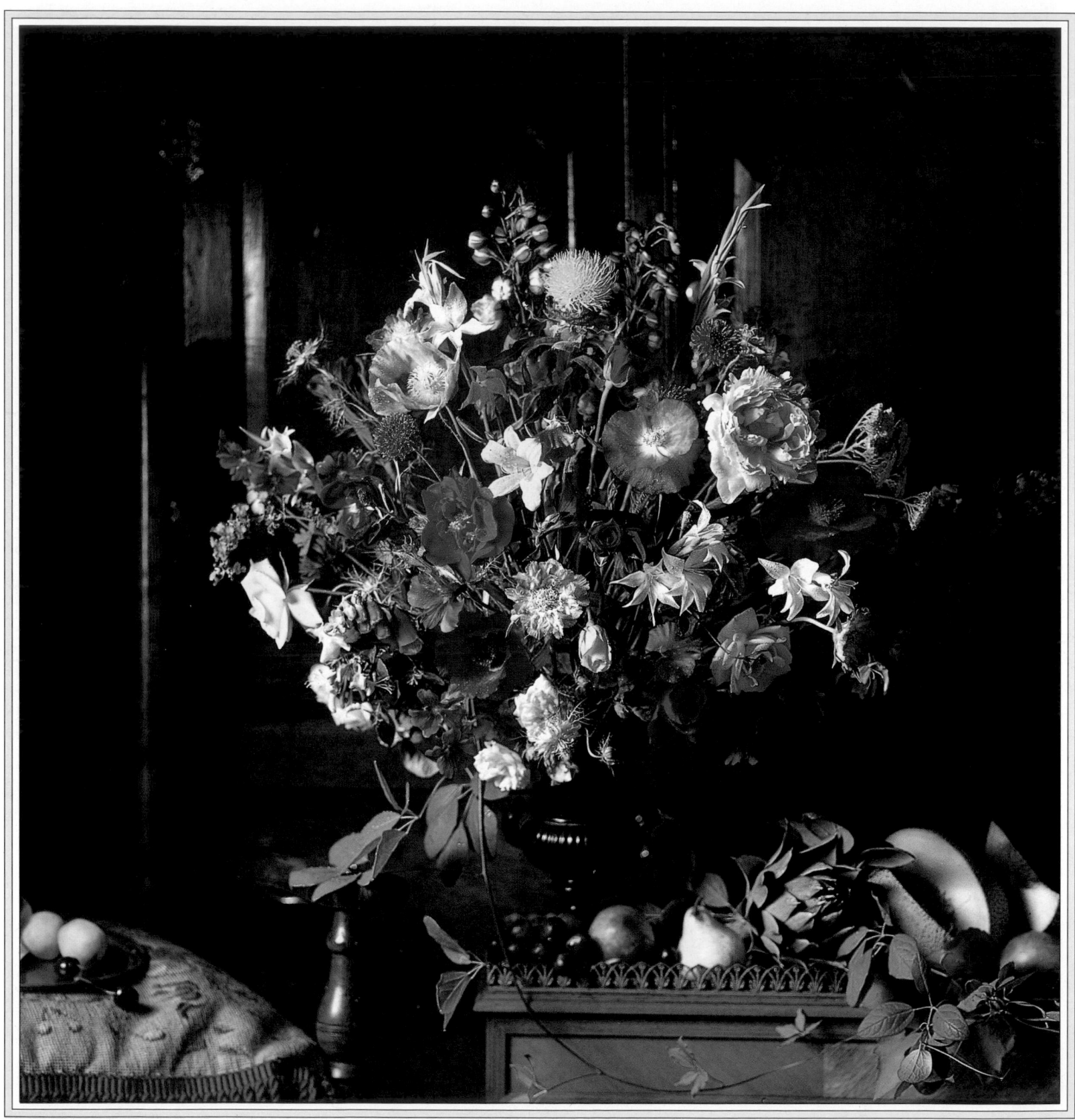

DUTCH MASTER

Delphiniums
Poppies
Cornflowers
Yellow knapweed (globe centaurea)
Roses
Foxgloves
Peonies
Daylilies (Hemerocallis)
Yarrow
Scabious (pincushion flower)
Love-in-a-mist
Alstroemeria
Mallow
White 'Alba' gladioli
Pinks (Dianthus x allwoodii)
Urn
Florists' foam

The richly detailed flower paintings of the 17th and 18th centuries can be recreated in your home in early summer when there is an abundance of flowers. This arrangement faces only one way, so place it against a wall. Choose flowers which have long, straight stems, in vivid colours with as near perfect blooms as possible.

First soak the foam well and pack it into the urn. This is a traditional triangular display, so begin by creating the outline. Use the longest-stemmed blooms — for example, the delphiniums — starting at the back of the display to provide the height and working down each side, keeping the line fairly symmetrical.

Mix the colours daringly, and work down the arrangement and out toward the sides with spiky gladioli, alstroemeria, mallow, cornflowers and love-in-a-mist.

Use the larger blooms — roses, poppies, daylilies and scabious — to fill the centre of the display and form the focal point.

Fill in any gaps with buds and remaining flowers. A little trailing foliage, such as honeysuckle, adds a touch of panache.

LEFT: The exquisite flower paintings of the 17th and 18th centuries provide an excellent source of ideas for flower arrangers today.

PRIMARY COLOURS

Variegated Pittosporum foliage
Gypsophila (baby's breath)
Yellow lilies
Holly berries (English holly)
Shallow blue glass bowl
Wire mesh

So often, it is the container that dictates the flowers you use. Here, the deep blue glass of this attractive 1930s bowl is offset by the bold yellows and reds of the flowers and berries, giving the whole display a striking note of primary colours.

First, make sure that the *Pittosporum* and holly (English holly) foliage has been well conditioned, otherwise it will deteriorate long before the rest of the display. Hammer the stems well and give them a long drink of water. (If you have trouble finding twigs with real berries, you can always cheat and use artificial ones.)

Squash the mesh into the bowl and fill it with water. Keeping a shallow outline, fill the bowl with stems of bushy *Pittosporum*. Intersperse stems of gypsophila (baby's breath) throughout the arrangement to relieve the density of the foliage.

Create the focal point with three open lilies, also adding a few buds.

Finally, position several twiggy pieces of holly, bearing as many berries as possible, throughout the display.

Bright blue glassware has inspired the use of primary colours and bold contours in this attractive display.

DRIED FLOWER DESIGNS

*Dried flowers are versatile, long-lasting and – if
preserved carefully – can retain the richness of
colour and beauty of form that they enjoy when
fresh. On the following pages, discover the best
way to preserve flowers and be inspired by dozens
of wonderfully different displays.*

In recent years the popularity of dried flowers has soared as the variety and availability of plant material has increased one-hundred fold. Specialist shops and an increasing number of florists now stock a wide variety of dried flowers, leaves and seedheads imported from all over the world.

But don't feel you have to buy all your dried material. Preserving your own can be immensely satisfying and enjoyable and the results can be as professional as anything you can buy in a shop.

BUYING DRIED FLOWERS

When buying dried flowers, make sure they are not dusty, dull specimens left over from the previous year. The best time to buy is in the autumn, soon after the fresh flower's natural season. Obviously, some flowers, and certainly leaves and seedheads, last very well. To check, make sure the colours are quite bright and not too faded, that the flower's foliage is a dull green and not a washed out grey and that none of the material is brittle or crumbling.

PRESERVING YOUR OWN

If you haven't a garden, try growing plants in patio tubs or window boxes. Or preserve bought fresh flowers. Market stalls are good places to buy inexpensive fresh flowers and many can be dried.

The cardinal rule is always to dry flowers in their prime. If you are picking garden flowers, choose a dry day just before the flowers are fully open and preferably in the middle of the day when the sap is rising. Shake off any dew and make sure that the petals are completely dry before you begin.

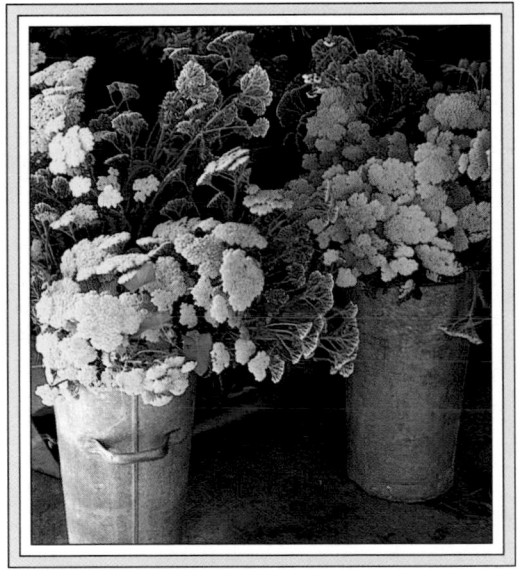

ABOVE: Yarrow – with its clusters of bright yellow flowers – is an easy plant to grow and it dries well.

LEFT: Always pick flowers in their prime. Choose a dry day and make sure the petals are free from dew or dampness. The best time for this is around midday

DRYING METHODS

There are several methods of preserving flowers but some plants can only successfully be dried by one method.

Air drying
One of the easiest drying methods is air drying. Many flowers can simply be left hanging upside down to dry in a dark, airy place such as an airing cupboard, attic or a spare room. It is important that the flowers are not put in direct sunlight as this will cause their colours to fade. You should first bind the flowers together in bunches before

hanging them. Rubber bands are best for this purpose as you will find that the stems shrink as they dry.

Suspend the flowers from a pole or some string and leave them till they are thoroughly dry. Particularly check the top of the stem, just below the flowerhead, because if this isn't dried out the flower will quickly droop when stood upright.

Some plants, such as sea lavender and pampas grass, dry best standing upright in a vase or jam jar. Others, like hydrangea, need to stand in a little water while they dry. Grasses and some seedheads dry best lying flat on newspaper. It is a good idea

Many flowers can be dried successfully by hanging them upside down in a shaded, airy place. Keep them out of direct sunlight as this will fade their colours.

to spray bushy grasses with hair spray as they have a tendency to explode and scatter their seeds everywhere.

Plants to air dry: sea lavender, lavender, statice, roses, love-in-a-mist, gypsophila (baby's breath), lady's mantle, delphinium, all seedheads and grasses, bottlebrush, sunray (Helipterum), helichrysum (strawflowers), Chinese lanterns and hops.

Glycerine

Most foliage is preserved using glycerine. Basically, the glycerine replaces the water in the leaves leaving them supple and leathery. Choose fresh foliage during the summer when the sap is still rising.

Hammer woody stems well so that they absorb the glycerine solution. The solution should be made from one part glycerine to two parts very hot water. Stir it well and stand the leaf sprays in about 3in (7.5cm) of the solution. This method can take about 10 days to four weeks. Wipe the leaves with a damp cloth if they begin to 'sweat'. If the leaves appear to wither and not absorb the solution, cut the stems back and try again.

Single leaves can also be preserved with glycerine by immersing them in a small dish of the solution. This should only take two or three days to work.

Plants to preserve with glycerine: virtually all green foliage can be preserved this way. However, silvered, downy or hairy leaves do not 'glycerine' well.

Desiccants

Desiccants — or drying agents — draw moisture from the plant and help to preserve the natural colours and form.

One of the simplest to use is silica gel, which can be bought from most hardware stores or chemists. It usually comes in white or blue crystals. The blue crystals will turn pink when they have absorbed water, so you will know when the plants are ready.

Put a layer of crystals in an airtight container and place several flowerheads on top (daisy types — face down, others — face up). Gently spoon more crystals on top to cover the flowers. Tightly secure the lid. Leave the flowers for a couple of days, then check; the petals should feel like tissue when they are ready.

Borax is cheaper than silica gel but it takes around 10 days to work. Ideally, it

Provided flowers stay out of any steam, they dry well when suspended above a solid fuel range, which gives out constant warmth.

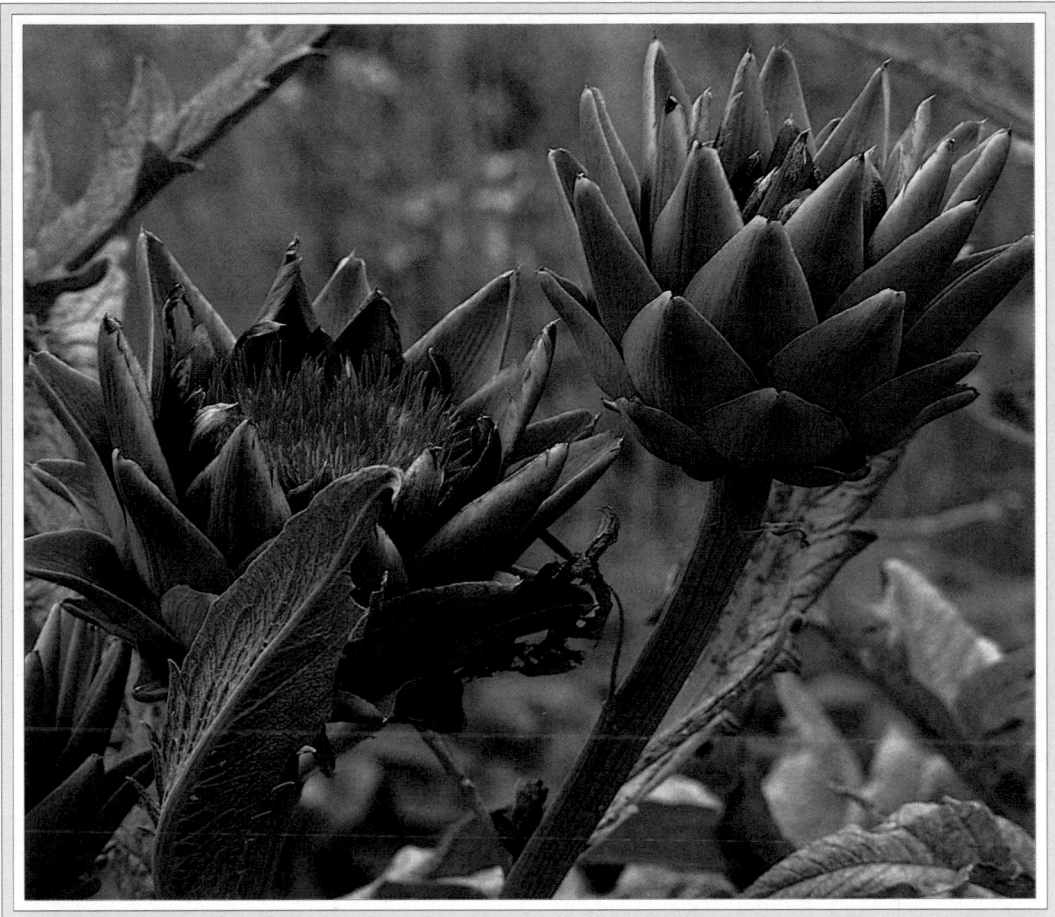

BASIC EQUIPMENT AND TECHNIQUES

Various items can be used to support dry flowers: florists' foam, specially designed for dry arrangements, is the most popular. It is grey in colour, comes in various shapes such as cones, tablets, spheres and bricks. and it can be cut easily to fit any container.

Wire mesh is also used to support larger displays. It can be crumpled or crushed into shape and packed with moss to form the base of a garland or pendant.

A variety of wire is used in dried flower arranging. Stub wires are straight lengths of wire used for supporting fragile flowers or binding small bunches of flowers together. They can also be used to support nuts and cones. Once wired, it is easy to insert these items into the foam base. Reel wire is finer and is used for more delicate work. U-pins are like wire hairpins and are used to attach various items into a display.

LEFT: *Many flowers can be given the desiccant treatment. A selection of perfect flower-heads lies in boxfuls of dessicant powder. More of the powder will be poured over and around each bloom before the lids are closed.*

BELOW: *You can give flowers more impact in a display by wiring them into small bunches before arranging them. First bend one end of a stub wire (a straight length of wire) into a hairpin or U-shape as shown.*

BELOW: *Cut the flower stems short and position them against the pin. Wind the long end of the wire about three times around the plant stems, then straighten it out to make a wire 'stem'.*

should be mixed with dry silver sand: three parts borax to two parts sand. Cover the flowers as with silica gel. To speed up the process you can use a microwave oven. But do make sure you check with your manufacturer's instructions beforehand. Cover the flowers with silica gel as before, but leave the container uncovered. Put it in the microwave oven together with a glass of water. Set to full power for 1-4 minutes depending on the fragility of the flower.

Flowers to preserve with desiccants: lily, cornflower, daffodil, daisy, freesia, pansy, hellebore, marigold, peony, rose and violet.

TANSY IN TERRACOTTA

Tansy
Wheat
Yarrow
Deep blue larkspur
Lavender
Sea holly or eryngo (Eryngium)
Old terracotta flower pot

This informal arrangement, displayed in a lovely weathered old flower pot, needs no mechanics to secure it.

Use plenty of tansy to form a dense outline. Add the taller plants and long stems of wheat to the back of the display. Push some shorter stems of wheat into the foreground. Fill in any gaps with clusters of sea holly. (Tansy can cause dermatitis so it's advisable to take care when using it.)

ABOVE: This Kitchen Spice Ball – with its exotic textures and shapes – is made from a range of spices and seedheads.

LEFT: Tansies are one of the easiest flowers to preserve. Their stems stay stiff and their colours remain true.

KITCHEN SPICE BALL

Cinnamon sticks
Spanish root (liquorice sticks)
Star anise
White lomius
Small and large poppy seedheads
Cones
Florists' dry foam sphere
Raffia
Stub wire

This aromatic pomander contains a range of interesting spices and seedheads and makes an attractive kitchen decoration.

Begin by plaiting three strands of raffia to form a hanging loop. Wire this into the dry foam sphere.

Make little bundles of cinnamon sticks and Spanish root and bind them with wire. Cover the wire with raffia strands. Wire the star anise and the lomius and cover the sphere with all these ingredients, trying to keep the display roughly spherical.

Now insert groups of large and small poppy seedheads into the remaining gaps.

To finish off your spice ball, add a few dark cones to give depth and substance to the display. The ones we used here are platyspernum cones.

FRAMED WITH FLOWERS

Clubrush (bulrush)
Yellow crepis (hawkbeard)
Bottlebrush flowers and foliage
White leaf skeletons
Picture frame
Tartan ribbon
Round tablet of florists' dry foam
Florists' tape

This attractive design illustrates how much a dried floral arrangement can enhance a plain picture frame — it's easy to do but so very effective.

Begin by slicing the foam into two round pieces and then taping them to two corners of the frame. Next, using single stems of clubrush, build up a loose spray shape. For a splash of colour, tuck in stems of crepis or other yellow plant, allowing some to trail across the frame and picture. Then insert a number of single stems of bottlebrush.

Once the sprays are complete, fill them out with plenty of bottlebrush foliage. Add highlights with a few leaf skeletons.

The tartan ribbon adds the finishing touch to the arrangement. Make two double bows and wire them into the sprays, balancing each corner of the picture frame.

HELICHRYSUM IN STONEWARE

Helichrysum (strawflowers)
Florists' dry foam
Old stoneware kitchen jars

Although quite an extravagant arrangement, these stunning helichrysum in bold reds, magentas and creamy yellows, will last for well over a year before fading.

To make one jarful of the flowers shown here, you will need almost 200 flowers. Of course, you can scale down the whole display and make a smaller arrangement in a smaller jar if you prefer.

If you are drying the helichrysum yourself, they will need their stems wired before they are dried. This is explained on page 39. You will find that most bought helichrysum are wired ready for use.

Pack the jar with foam and begin with a flower in the centre. As a guide, it should be slightly taller than the height of the jar. Now insert more helichrysum to form a dome shaped outline, letting ones toward the rim of the jar drape over the edge. The easiest way to achieve an even outline is to keep turning the jar and inserting the flowers at intervals until you have established a strong shape. You can then fill in the gaps with more helichrysum.

Jars of glowing helichrysum (strawflowers) make a bold mantelpiece decoration that will last for many months.

ABOVE: Vibrant yellow flowers set into this little pomander bring a touch of sunshine into the bedroom.

GOLDEN POMANDER

Small yellow helichrysum (strawflowers)
Florists' dry foam sphere
Ribbon
Stub wire

You can hang this pretty pomander from a dressing table or wardrobe door for a feminine touch to a bedroom.

First, make a loop from the ribbon and wire it into the sphere, pushing the wire right through to the base. Trim the wire and then bend the end back into the foam.

Next, insert the helichrysum, packing the flowers tightly into the ball and keeping them all at the same height to maintain the round shape.

Finish with a double bow, wiring it into the top of the pomander.

A WINTER'S WREATH

Sea lavender
Purple statice
Yarrow
Tiny clustered sunray (Helipterum)
Cones
Moss wreath
Stub wire

This attractive winter's wreath in muted creams and golds with a dash of purple makes a delightfully natural decoration to hang on your door. The added bonus is that this combination of flowers and cones is remarkably inexpensive to assemble.

Wire together clumps of sea lavender and virtually cover the entire moss wreath with it. Next, take some purple statice and wire together several bunches. Intersperse the purple statice evenly amongst the sea lavender and then, at regular intervals, insert some wired clumps of yarrow and sunray. Gather about 10-12 large cones and wire them together in a large bunch. With more wire fix the cones to the base of the wreath. Pull a few strands of flowers between the cones to help offset them.

To finish, intersperse a few more of the cones throughout the wreath to add an interesting contrast of tone and texture to your winter arrangement.

BELOW: Clusters of gold and cream flowers form the basis of this lovely Winter's Wreath.

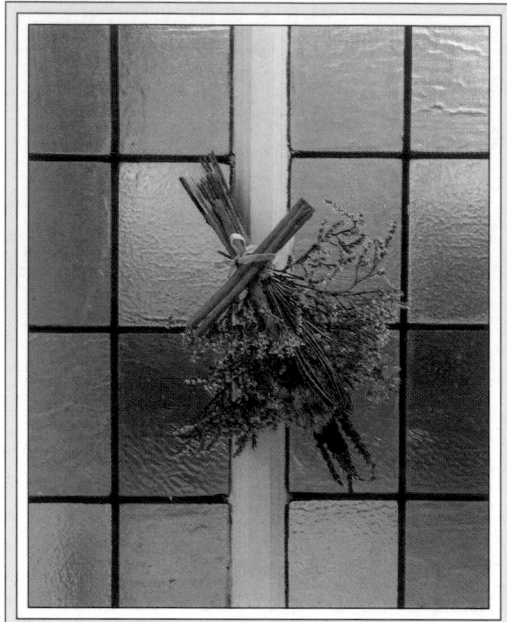

Herbs and flowers make an attractive decoration for a front door or pretty window.

HANGING BUNCH

Lavender
Southernwood
Rosemary
Ornamental onion
Cinnamon sticks
Sea lavender
Reel wire
Raffia

Small bunches of herbs and flowers were once used to repel insects and moths. Today, such bunches have lost none of their properties and they look decorative too. Lavender can also be used on its own, bunched into a 'bottle' (see page 145).

Gather the herbs, ornamental onion and sea lavender into an attractive bunch and wire the stems together securely. Next, wire together two or three cinnamon sticks and bind these on to the bunch, aligning them with the stems. Wire more cinnamon sticks together and set these across the first bunch. Finally, cover any visible wires with raffia strands and finish off with a raffia loop to hang the bunch up.

SILVER POSY

Lily of the valley
Grape hyacinths
Cornflowers
Pansies
Astrantia
Narcissi
Pulmonaria
Spurge
Salad burnet (garden burnet) leaves
Silver bowl
Florists' stub wire
Wire mesh

All the flowers in this pretty miniature display have been carefully preserved in silica gel (see page 37 for details). This method of preservation retains the colour and form of the flowers well, and for more delicate specimens, such as narcissi, it is the only preservation method suitable.

Once preserved, it is best to strengthen the delicate stems by wiring them.

Fill the bowl with crushed wire mesh and gently insert the wired flowers to build up a triangular shape. Use the pansies as the focal flowers. Dried foliage can be added to hide any visible wires.

LILAC NET

Red amaranthus (love-lies-bleeding)
Blue larkspur
Soft pink, cluster-flowered
helichrysum (strawflowers)
Basket with handle
Pot-pourri (for recipes, see pages 87-97)
Lilac coloured netting
Stub wire

Soft net has been used here to create a soft, billowing effect.

Wire together clumps of amaranthus and insert them at intervals around the rim of the basket. Angle them for more interest.

Fill in the display with clusters of larkspur and helichrysum sprays, forming a dense ring of flowers around the basket. Now tie bows of lilac net to the basket handle and fill the bowl with pot-pourri.

RIGHT: It is difficult to believe that all the flowers in this pretty Silver Posy are preserved and not fresh.

BELOW: Lilac net brings out the blues and purples of this lovely pot-pourri basket.

ABOVE: This decorative nosegay also has the practical purpose of repelling moths.

MOTH REPELLENT NOSEGAY

Dried lavender
Lavender bottles (see page 145)
Roses
Southernwood
Nipplewort
Wire
Velvet ribbon

Dried flowers and herbs have been used for centuries to keep harmful insects away from susceptible fabrics. This particular design is ideal for keeping moths at bay, and is pretty enough to use as a decoration in its own right, hung on the back of a bedroom door, for example.

To make the bunch, simply bind all the flowers together with wire. Tie some velvet ribbon around the stems and form it into a loop for hanging the nosegay.

As well as lavender and southernwood, other plants you could use for repelling moths include sea lavender, lady's mantle and sprigs of rosemary. Roses and other pretty flowers can also be added for decorative purposes.

COFFEE SACKS

Yellow and beige sea lavender
Wild oats
Phalaris
Wheat
Ornamental onion
Bells of Ireland
Brown plants such as Ti-tree,
Leptocarpus, Gynerium, Carex pendula
Rust coloured eucalyptus
Teasels
Safflowers
Sorrel
Sunray (Helipterum)
Yarrow
Tiny cones
Small coffee sacks
Florists' dry foam
Crumpled newspaper or tissue paper

The rough hessian of coffee sacks provides a good backdrop for these natural displays. You can experiment with any number of reeds, dried grasses and cereal plants in their natural colours. Any other brown, beige or rust coloured plants will also complement well. Touches of colour here and there to lift the displays are provided by the orange tips of the safflowers and the cheerful white heads of the sunrays.

Push a brick of florists' foam into the sack and pack the sack out with tissue paper or crumpled newspaper.

In one sack, form a softly curving outline with the grasses, wired cones and foliage,

until you have a dense display. Fill in the centre with the safflowers and yarrow.

The second sack achieves a different effect using beige sea lavender, a sweeping spray of teasels and some striking white sunrays. Follow the lines shown here to create a well-balanced arrangement.

BELOW: A medley of grasses, seedheads and cereals in plain coffee sacks echo the simple beauty of the hedgerow.

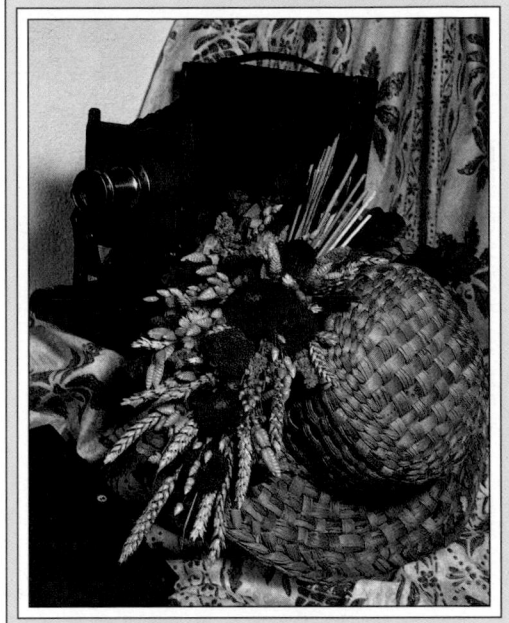

ABOVE: This straw hat makes a pretty, decorative feature when adorned with sprays of wheat and dahlias.

EDWARDIAN HAT

Orange dahlias
Helichrysum (strawflowers)
Golden rod
Wheat
Dryandra
Quaking grass
Oak foliage
Straw hat
Moss
Reel and stub wire
All-purpose glue and wreath wrap

Try livening up a plain straw boater with this striking floral spray.

Mould the moss into an egg shape and bind it with reel wire. Cover the shape with wreath wrap and secure it to the hat, again with reel wire threaded through the weave.

Cut the wheat stems and save the stalks. Wire the ears into clumps and push them into the moss. Wire in dahlias, helichrysum and oak leaves. Bunch the discarded wheat stems and wire these into one end. Finally, glue leaves around one side of the brim.

FLOWER TREE

*Orange and yellow
helichrysum (strawflowers)
Blue larkspur
Green amaranthus (love-lies-bleeding)
Plastic pot for base
Plaster of Paris
Interesting short, thick branch or
branches for the trunk
Wire mesh
Dry sphagnum moss
Twigs
U-pins
Raffia
Florists' dry foam sphere
Stub wire
Bun moss*

This ever-popular form of floral arrangement is easier to achieve than it looks.

Mix the plaster of Paris with water and pour it into the plastic container. Quickly insert the branch, which will act as the tree trunk, and hold it in position until the plaster has set sufficiently. Leave the plaster to dry for several hours.

Next, form a ring of wire mesh, slightly deeper than the container and wide enough to fit snugly around it. The ring must be double thickness so you can pack it tightly with the dry sphagnum moss. When it is fully packed, neatly bend the raw edges of wire over to close the ring.

Cut the twigs into equal lengths, the depth of the moss ring, and attach them with two U-pins per twig. Cover the pins with two lengths of raffia.

Place the container with the tree trunk inside the wire surround. Take the foam sphere and scrape out a hole for the trunk. Push the sphere down hard on to the trunk, making sure it is held firm.

Decorate the tree by wiring the helichrysum into small bunches and inserting them evenly around the sphere. Keep the tree

LEFT: Don't be daunted – this stunning and colourful flower tree is quite straight-forward to assemble.

52

ABOVE: Rich rusty coloured roses and creamy sunray spill out of a jet black wooden box.

turning to create a round shape. Next, add the larkspur and the amaranthus, tucking them in to retain a neat, spherical shape.

Finish off with a few pieces of bun moss around the base of the tree to hide the plaster and the wire mesh.

LAVENDER WALL DISPLAY

Canary grass
Lavender
Flat-backed wall basket
Florists' dry foam
Plastic coated florists' wire
Knife
All-purpose glue or hot glue gun

Inspired by Elizabethan garden engravings, this attractive wall design is built up by arranging alternate rows of lavender and canary grass.

Fill the wall basket with the florists' dry foam, then trim the foam into a convex shape with a knife.

Cut the canary grass stems to approximately 1in (2.5cm) and insert them around the bottom edge of the basket. Next insert

RIGHT: Rows of canary grass and lavender create a striking wall display.

four rows of lavender and, keeping to the shape of the basket, add another row of canary grass. Work another few rows of lavender, one of canary grass and finish with more lavender.

For a final decorative touch, you can wire together a few stems of the lavender and canary grass into a small bunch and glue it to the front of the basket.

LATE SUMMER ROSES

Bupleurum
Cream sunray (Helipterum)
Rust coloured roses
Black, wooden box
Florists' dry foam

A jet black wooden box provides a frame for this pretty arrangement and helps to bring out the subtle warmth of the roses.

First, cut the florists' foam to fit snugly inside the box. Insert clumps of bupleurum to form the outline and help prop open the lid of the box. Use shorter stems at the front so that they slightly overhang the edge of the box. Fill in the outline with the cream coloured sunray.

Complete the picture with the roses. First, gently steam some of them. This will soften the petals a little so that you can then pull back the outer ones to open out the flowers before you position them.

For the best effect, recess some of the roses deep into the display, keeping one or two more prominent.

NUT AND CONE ROPE

Cones
Walnuts
Chinese lanterns
Quaking grass
Stub wire
Wide gold giftwrap ribbon

The framework of this seasonal garland is made of cones and walnuts. Wire each cone by wrapping a stub wire around its base. For each walnut, push a stub wire through one end as far as it will go.

Take a group of nuts and cones and twist the wires together. Add to the base of the group with more cones and nuts, twisting the wires together to secure each group. Continue adding cones and nuts in this way until the 'rope' is long enough.

Using the giftwrap ribbon, make a double bow for the top of the rope, adding some additional tails for fullness. Wire this into the display.

Just behind the bow, wire in a long length of ribbon and twist this in and out of the rope until you reach the end; leave a long tail trailing. Cut a swallowtail into the end of the ribbon for a neat finish.

Finally, wire together small groups of Chinese lanterns and quaking grass and intersperse these amongst the cones, entangling the wires to secure them.

LIGHTS AND STARS

Reddish-bronze hydrangeas
Poppy seedheads
Globe artichokes (optional)
Shallow basket with handle
Bronze or copper jug
Silver spray paint
Florists' dry foam
Gold cord
Silver glitter stars

ABOVE: This attractive Nut and Cone Rope, with its swirling gold ribbon, makes an ideal Christmas decoration. Change the ribbon for a year-round hanging display.

Silver and gold look rich and festive and, mixed with the subtle colours of dried hydrangea flowerheads, they make a luxurious Christmas arrangement. First, spray the hydrangea heads lightly with silver paint, just enough to frost them without obscuring their natural colour. They will not take long to dry.

In the meantime, wedge a block of florists' dry foam into the basket. Push the silvery hydrangeas into the basket and fill in any gaps with poppy seedheads and add a spiky artichoke head or two if you wish. Tie a gold cord bow on to the handle of the basket for the finishing touch.

For the jug, you will need no mechanics. Simply fill it with silvery hydrangeas and

ABOVE: Use lengths of wide tartan ribbon, tied into generous bows, to create this charming Scottish garland. Clusters of red roses and cream pearl everlasting pick out the colours in the tartan.

ABOVE: Dried hydrangea heads, lightly highlighted with silver, form the basis of this sumptuous Christmas arrangement.

add some silver glitter stars. (These can be bought, or you could make your own from metallic cardboard, glitter and wire).

Offset the whole display with a shallow dish of floating candles wrapped in gold filigree ribbon, a selection of shiny baubles and some burnished trinket boxes.

SCOTTISH SALUTE

Red roses
Pearl everlasting (Anaphalis)
Twig ring
Stub wire
Wide tartan ribbon

A slightly different festive garland, this design makes the perfect accompaniment to a tartan-trimmed Christmas tree. Wire the roses individually and set them in three

small groups into the ring. Now wire together nine small bunches of pearl everlasting and push them into the ring so that they surround the roses.

Complete the garland with the ribbon. Tie three lengths into generous single bows and wire them into the three spaces on the ring. For the ribbon tails, cut one more length of ribbon, fold it in half and push a piece of wire through the folded end. Trim the two ends into swallowtails and wire this beneath one of the bows.

YELLOW MELON

Daffodils
Purple hyacinths
Jonquil
Three double white tulips
Stems of eucalyptus
Honeydew melon
Florists' foam

Fruit and flowers make great companions for any buffet or dinner table. Here, a golden honeydew melon makes a practical and pretty container for the flowers.

First, cut a wedge from the melon and scoop out most of the flesh, putting it into the refrigerator to eat later. Then push a piece of soaked florists' foam into the fruit and insert stems of eucalyptus to create an asymmetrical outline.

Now you can arrange the flowers. Begin by cutting the daffodil stems on a slant to make them easier to insert into the foam. Cut one daffodil shorter than the rest and put it in the foreground as the focal flower. Position the other daffodils at increasing heights on one side of the display.

Insert the jonquil to the other side. Bring some through the front of the display and place a couple behind the focal daffodil. Add the hyacinths next and complete the display with the white tulips.

YELLOW ROSE BOWL

Yellow roses
Yellow freesias
Cream spider chrysanthemums
Leucodendron foliage
Silver rose bowl
Wire mesh (if necessary)

Little can beat a traditional rose arrangement set in a silver bowl in the centre of a highly polished dining table.

A traditional rose bowl should have a wire mesh centre to support the blooms; if not, crush some wire mesh and push this into the bowl.

Fill the bowl with water and pack it with the chrysanthemums, cutting the stems short to give a dense base for the other flowers. Then, place the roses in between the chrysanthemums, keeping the stems a little longer. Next, intersperse the arrangement with a few freesias.

Finally, add the *Leucodendron* foliage and freesia buds, ensuring that the stems are slightly longer than those of the other flowers. A full-blown rose at the foot of the bowl will complete the arrangement and last for the duration of the dinner party.

BELOW: Large fruits, such as this melon, make ideal containers for flowers.

ABOVE: Rose bowls are designed to show roses off to their best advantage, as this charming yellow arrangement demonstrates.

LEMON PYRAMID

Lemon roses
Yellow lilies and buds
White stock
Plate
Florists' foam cone

This stunning display makes a wonderful accompaniment to a wedding buffet table or special occasion party. It is also conveniently quick to assemble.

Soak the florists' foam well and stand it on the plate. It should be heavy enough not to need fixing.

Begin with the lilies. Snip out their pollen-laden stamens, which severely stain when brushed against furniture or clothing. Cut their stalks down to about 2in (5cm) and insert the first one into the top of the cone. Work down the sides of the cone, angling each flowerhead slightly for interest. Now add the roses, spacing them out evenly between the lilies. Finally, fill in with short stems of sweet smelling stock.

RIGHT: Pyramid arrangements, such as this Lemon Pyramid, are perfect for buffet tables as they can be clearly seen above the food.

SPRINGTIME BUFFET

Pink hyacinths
White daffodils
Grape hyacinths (Muscari)
Serving dish or cake stand
Wire mesh
Florists' foam cone
Water resistant tape

This elegant serving dish is perfect for a pyramid flower design and makes a superb decoration for a buffet table.

Wrap the foam cone in wire mesh and attach the cone to the dish with the tape. Now soak the cone well with water.

Insert a hyacinth bud at the top of the cone and, turning the dish around, add the remaining hyacinths, graduating in size down toward the edge of the dish to create the pyramid shape.

Tuck in white daffodils between the sprays of hyacinths and finally add the rich blue grape hyacinths to define the shape and provide colour contrast.

ABOVE: Dark green ivy provides the foil for the candles and cream freesias in this stylish centrepiece.

LEFT: A collection of hyacinths and daffodils, this delightful springtime arrangement will enhance any special occasion buffet table.

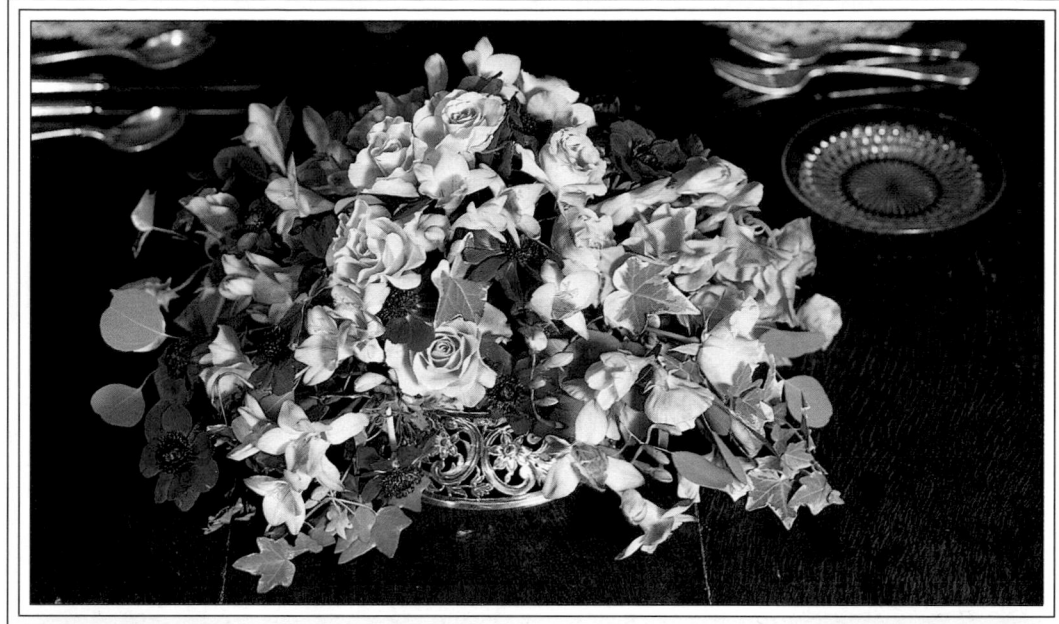

ABOVE: The subtle colours and low-lying arrangement make Harmony an elegant and stylish dinner party centrepiece.

IVY CANDLE RING

White freesias
Trailing ivy stems
Circular cake base
Drawing pins
Modelling clay or florists' putty
Selection of white and green candles

This attractive candle ring, with its elegant dark green and white colour scheme, will suit any special occasion. Make this display on the evening of the event as the ivy withers if kept too long. In order to keep the freesias fresh you can bind the stem ends with a little wet cotton wool.

Begin by attaching strands of ivy to the edge of the cake base with drawing pins. Build up the ring by adding more strands and bunches of leaves until only a small space remains in the centre. Insert stems of freesia among the ivy leaves to provide colour contrast. Push blobs of modelling clay or florists' putty into the centre of the display and insert a mixture of white and green candles of varying heights.

HARMONY

Mauve freesias
Mauve roses
Mauve sweet peas
Purple anemones
Ivy
Eucalyptus foliage
Silver dish
Glass bowl
Florists' foam and tape

The beautiful floral fretwork on the silver dish used for this arrangement looks stunning against the dark wood of the dining table and harmonizes well with the mauve and purple blooms.

Place a glass bowl filled with foam inside your silver dish and secure the foam with florists' tape. Soak the foam well with water. Place stems of the different leaves around the edge of the dish, allowing the ivy to trail on to the table.

Insert a rose in the centre of the bowl and position the remaining roses to graduate down to the rim of the dish. Add the sweet peas, freesias and dark anemones among the roses, letting these, like the ivy, also trail on to the table. Finish off with an occasional ivy leaf peeping through the flowers to add to the display.

DANCING LIGHTS

Golden orange chrysanthemum heads
Shallow glass dish
Floating yellow candles

One of the simplest table displays — floating candles and flowerheads — can also be the most effective. The candlelights dance on the water giving a flattering light to any dinner or supper party.

Fill a shallow glass pie or fruit dish with water and add four or five floating candles. Float 12-14 chrysanthemum flowerheads alongside the candles.

Light the candles when you are ready to eat; they last at least four hours.

HARVEST NAPKIN

A few dried stems of canary grass
Stems of wheat
Dried orange statice
Straw placemat
White napkin
1¾ yd (1.5 metres) of beige ribbon
Thread

This simple place setting makes an attractive accompaniment to any Thanksgiving or Harvest supper table.

Cut the ribbon into three equal lengths and tie these together at one end. Plait them until the plait is long enough to tie around the napkin twice with a little left over.

In Dancing Lights, a glass dish gives maximum sparkle to bobbing candles and floating flowerheads.

Next, group the wheat, grasses and statice together and secure them with a piece of thread or fine wire.

Then fold the napkin in half twice to form a long, thin rectangle. Lay the flowers on top of the napkin and wind the plaited ribbon around the napkin and the flowers twice, tying the ends under the napkin.

For added variety, you could match the plaited ribbon to the colour of the statice. For a less autumnal look, use purple or blue statice instead of the orange.

ABOVE: Cake stands make excellent table centrepieces. The brightly coloured flowers used here have been assembled to resemble a rich gateau.

BELOW: Complement a scrubbed pine table and straw placemats with this natural Harvest Napkin tie.

RUSTIC CENTREPIECE

Cones
Walnuts
Preserved oak leaves
Dried winged everlasting or sandflowers (Ammobium)
Small cork mat or cake base
Small block of dry florists' foam
Florists' wire
Florists' tape
White candle

This woodland design using nuts, cones and leaves makes the perfect centrepiece for a stripped pine or plain wooden table, especially in a country kitchen.

Begin by taping a block of dry florists' foam on to a small cork mat or cake base. Wire up several cones and walnuts, forcing the wire through the base of each nut as far as it will go.

Wire together clumps of oak leaves and build up the outline of the display. Now insert the nuts and cones, placing the walnuts in small clusters. Keep the shape irregular to make it more interesting.

Brighten the display by scattering small clumps of winged everlasting throughout. To finish, trim a candle to the required length and push it firmly into the foam.

FLORAL GATEAU

Yellow roses
Alstroemeria
Leucodendron brunia
Red ranunculus
Mimosa
Coloured glass cake stand
Florists' foam

This sumptious arrangement of plump flowers on a glass cake stand looks almost edible. To make sure that this display lasts, condition the flowers before you arrange them (see pages 148-151 for details).

Soak the piece of florists' foam well and place it in the centre of the stand. Insert the roses and alstroemeria alternately around the edge of the foam; keep the stems short so that when inserted into the foam the flowerheads rest on the edge of the dish.

The next layer is created with bobbly *Leucodendron brunia* flowers. Above this, place your layer of bright red ranunculus. Finally, top the 'gateau' with a few sprays of brilliant yellow mimosa.

BELOW: The warm browns of autumn come together in this lovely Rustic Centrepiece, perfect for a cosy supper party.

$\mathscr{P}$RESSED FLOWERS

Pressed flowers made into a simple picture are shown off to perfection in an antique frame.

The art of pressing flowers is yet another absorbing pastime to be enjoyed from growing, gathering and collecting flowers and foliage. By pressing flowers, you will have the perfect medium for creating pictures and patterns of lasting beauty. You can turn them into gifts or treasures for your own home.

 72

here's a multitude of plant material you can press successfully. If you are careful how you press, the colour and form of the original plant can be captured for lasting pleasure.

WHAT TO SELECT

Annuals, perennials, shrubs and trees — whether from the garden, patio or florist — all provide material for pressing. Even if you only have a window box, you can sow alyssum, candytuft, forget-me-nots, lobelia and polyanthus.

There's also a huge range of common wild flowers, leaves and grasses to be gathered on a country walk. But do take care. Don't break off stems or pull up root: cleanly cut the parts you require with scissors. And do pay attention to the official list of protected plants that you may not pick.

It is worth attempting to press almost anything: don't forget tendrils, interesting stems, grasses and seedheads. The only types to avoid are succulent and fleshy flowers as these contain too much moisture to press successfully.

WHEN TO PICK AND PRESS

The best time to pick flowers for pressing is toward midday when all the dew has evaporated. Sunny weather is best and rainy days should be avoided. If you have to pick flowers when the weather is damp, pick whole stems, and stand them indoors in water until the petals are dry. Choose flowers that have just opened and before they have produced pollen, but gather some buds as well.

The same goes for bought flowers. Don't be tempted to enjoy them first, but press them when they are at their best. You also need to be aware of varying sizes, unusual shapes, a variety of tints and veining and interesting visual textures, as these are the elements that will not be lost in preserving.

Remember as you are pressing that you can thin out collective flowerheads such as candytuft, wild parsley and hydrangea, so don't pass over large-headed flowers in the belief that they won't press well. Multi-petalled or thick-centred flowers, such as roses, carnations and marguerites, will also need to be broken down into separate parts for pressing. Their parts can be used individually or they can be reassembled to their more familiar form.

BELOW: Small flowers, such as primroses and forget-me-nots, are ideal for pressing. Pick them toward midday on a sunny day.

MOIST POT-POURRI

10 cups of partially dried rose petals
3 cups of coarse salt
2 tbsp of ground cinnamon
2 tbsp of ground allspice
2 tbsp of ground nutmeg
1 tbsp of ground cloves
5 tbsp of orris root powder
3 or 4 drops of rose essential oil

This pot-pourri is made from roses only, but other scented flowers can be added with the spices. If you decide to do this, these additional flowers should always be fully dried.

The finished mixture is basically brown and not very attractive, but the scent is superb. Disguise the dull colour with a few whole roseheads.

The rose petals should be partially dried so that they feel leathery. Place some of the petals in a large bowl, cover them with a layer of coarse salt and continue to add layers of petals and salt until you have used up all the ingredients. Put a plate on top of the mixture in order to weigh it down. Stir the ingredients every day, to be sure that you are draining off any moisture.

After three to six weeks, crumble the mixture and add to it the spices, the rose essential oil and orris root powder. Seal the mix in paper bags and cure it for about six weeks before using.

Disguise the rather unappealing colours of Moist Pot-Pourri by piling it into a pretty basket, and adding whole, dried roseheads.

ABOVE: This attractive pink and red Rosebud pot-pourri is enhanced with cornflower petals and larkspur.

TRADITIONAL ROSE POT-POURRI

*2 cups of dried strongly scented rose petals
1 cup of dried lavender
½ cup of dried marjoram
1 tbsp of cloves
½ cup of dried orange peel (zest)
6 nutmegs
3-4 broken cinnamon sticks
3 tbsp of orris root powder
4 or 5 drops of rose essential oil*

This traditional English country recipe combines the wonderful fragrances of roses, orange and cinnamon.

Mix all the dried ingredients together in a large bowl. Add three tablespoons of orris root powder and stir thoroughly. Now carefully stir in the rose essential oil using a metal spoon. When the pot-pourri is well mixed put it into an airtight container and leave for four to six weeks, shaking the mixture occasionally.

RIGHT: Musky spices and deep-scented rose petals combine in this Traditional Rose Pot-Pourri.

ROSEBUDS

*4 cups of dried red or deep pink rose petals
1 cup of whole pink or red dried rosebuds
1 cup of dried lavender flowers
A few dried cornflower petals
Whole dried peonies (optional)
4 tbsp of orris root powder
1 tbsp of ground allspice
1 tbsp of ground cinnamon
1 tbsp of ground nutmeg
½ tbsp of ground cloves
4 or 5 drops of rose essential oil*

Dried rosebuds are the perfect complement to a traditional rose petal pot-pourri mixture. For additional interest, add two or three larger blooms, such as open roseheads or peonies.

Combine all the dry ingredients in a large bowl, sifting and mixing them well with your fingers. Stir in the orris root powder then, using a metal spoon, carefully add the rose essential oil.

Transfer the mixture to a sealed container and leave to cure in a cool, dark place for six weeks. Shake the mixture occasionally.

BURNING BUNDLES

*Stalks from dried lavender, rosemary,
thyme and lemon verbena
Twigs
Pine or larch cones, preferably still
on their twigs
String*

Although not strictly pot-pourri, these bundles of aromatic twigs, stalks and cones scent the room beautifully when burned on an open fire. They make good use of the stripped stalks you might have left over from making more traditional pot-pourri. Scattered across the fireplace or stored in open baskets, they look most attractive.

Gather the aromatic stalks, twigs and cones into small bundles and tie them with pieces of string. Hang them up or place them in shallow baskets close to the fire.

FOREST WALK

*3 cups of well-dried pinewood shavings
3 cups of small pine cones
2 cups of mixed nuts
1 cup of acorns, well dried
1 cup of cinnamon bark
1 cup of dried golden rod or yellow statice
2 tsp of dried orange peel (zest)
1/2 cup of bay leaves
1 tsp of mixed spice
5 tbsp of orris root powder
6 or 8 drops of pine essential oil*

This mixture will fill your room with an invigorating pine fragrance. Bowls of this pot-pourri can look very effective when displayed with a handful of acorns and yellow flowerheads scattered on top.

Before you begin, check that all your ingredients are completely dried out. This applies especially to the wood shavings and the acorns which could attract mildew

*LEFT: Fragrant twigs and sticks are gathered
into Burning Bundles ready to be placed
on an open fire.*

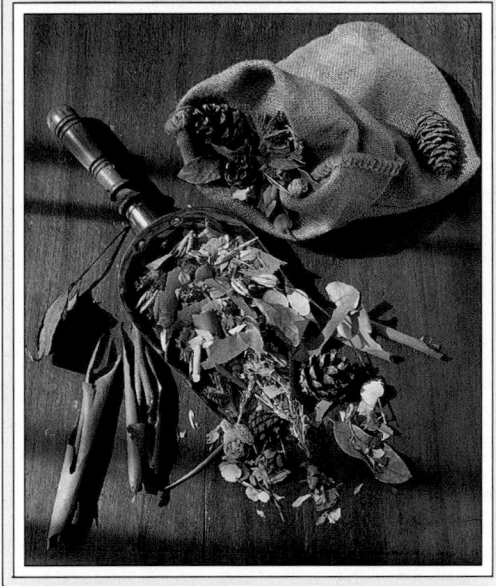

*ABOVE: The chunky textures and woodland
tones of Forest Walk create a more masculine
pot-pourri – perfect for a study or bedroom.*

mould if they are not thoroughly dry. Discard anything if it shows any trace of damp before you prepare the pot-pourri.

Mix all the dried items together in a large bowl. Next, add two or three drops of pine essential oil. Mix well, then transfer to dry airtight containers for six weeks, shaking occasionally while the mixture is curing.

NATURE'S FRUITS

*1 cup of peach stones
1 cup of rose hips
1 cup of beech masts (nuts)
1 cup of larch cones
1 cup of star anise
3 or 4 whole or cracked nutmegs
6 broken cinnamon sticks
1 cup of dried apple slices
4 tbsp of orris root powder
3 drops of allspice essential oil
3 drops of sweet orange essential oil*

This wintery mixture of spices, cones and fruit makes an unusual pot-pourri. You can dry the apple slices by placing them on a baking sheet and leaving them for several hours at the bottom of an oven set at a very low temperature.

With the exception of the apples, orris root and oil, mix all the ingredients together in a large bowl. Add the orris root powder to the mixture and stir in the essential oil, drop by drop. When the ingredients are thoroughly mixed, stir in the apple. Place the pot-pourri in an airtight container for about a month, shaking it regularly.

*BELOW: The fruit and spice mix of Nature's
Fruits looks best displayed in a shallow bowl.*

ABOVE: The shells used in Ocean Fragrance can be collected from the beach or bought from a shell or craft shop.

BELOW: Spring Selection has plenty of whole flowerheads for texture, including roses, marigolds, mimosa and helichrysum (strawflowers). For interest, add a bunch of cinnamon sticks.

OCEAN FRAGRANCE

1 cup of assorted shells
½ cup of dried oak moss
6 cinnamon sticks
1 cup of dried blue larkspur flowers
A few love-in-the-mist seedheads
and beech masts (nuts)
2 tbsp of orris root powder
4 drops of essential oil of your choice

Perfect for any bathroom, this seashell pot-pourri can be scented just as you wish, although a spicy or woody fragrance is probably more suitable than a floral one.

Place all the dried ingredients and the shells into a large bowl and mix them together well. Add the orris root powder and mix in. Finally, add the essential oil and stir in until all the oil is absorbed.

Put the mixture into an airtight container and leave for four to six weeks, giving it an occasional shake.

SPRING SELECTION

1 cup of dried chamomile flowers
½ cup of dried marigold petals
½ cup of dried lemon verbena leaves
1 cup of dried mixed yellow flowers,
eg mimosa, tulip, daffodil
A few whole dried yellow chilli peppers,
marigold heads or cinnamon
sticks for decoration
2 tsp of ground coriander
2 tsp of ground cinnamon
2 tbsp of orris root powder
4 drops of vetivert essential oil

This light, lemony, pot-pourri will give you a delightful mixture for spring.

Mix the petals, flowers and leaves in a large bowl. Add the spices and orris root, stirring well. Drip the essential oil into the mixture, and stir well with a metal spoon. Put into a sealed container, and leave for four to six weeks, shaking occasionally.

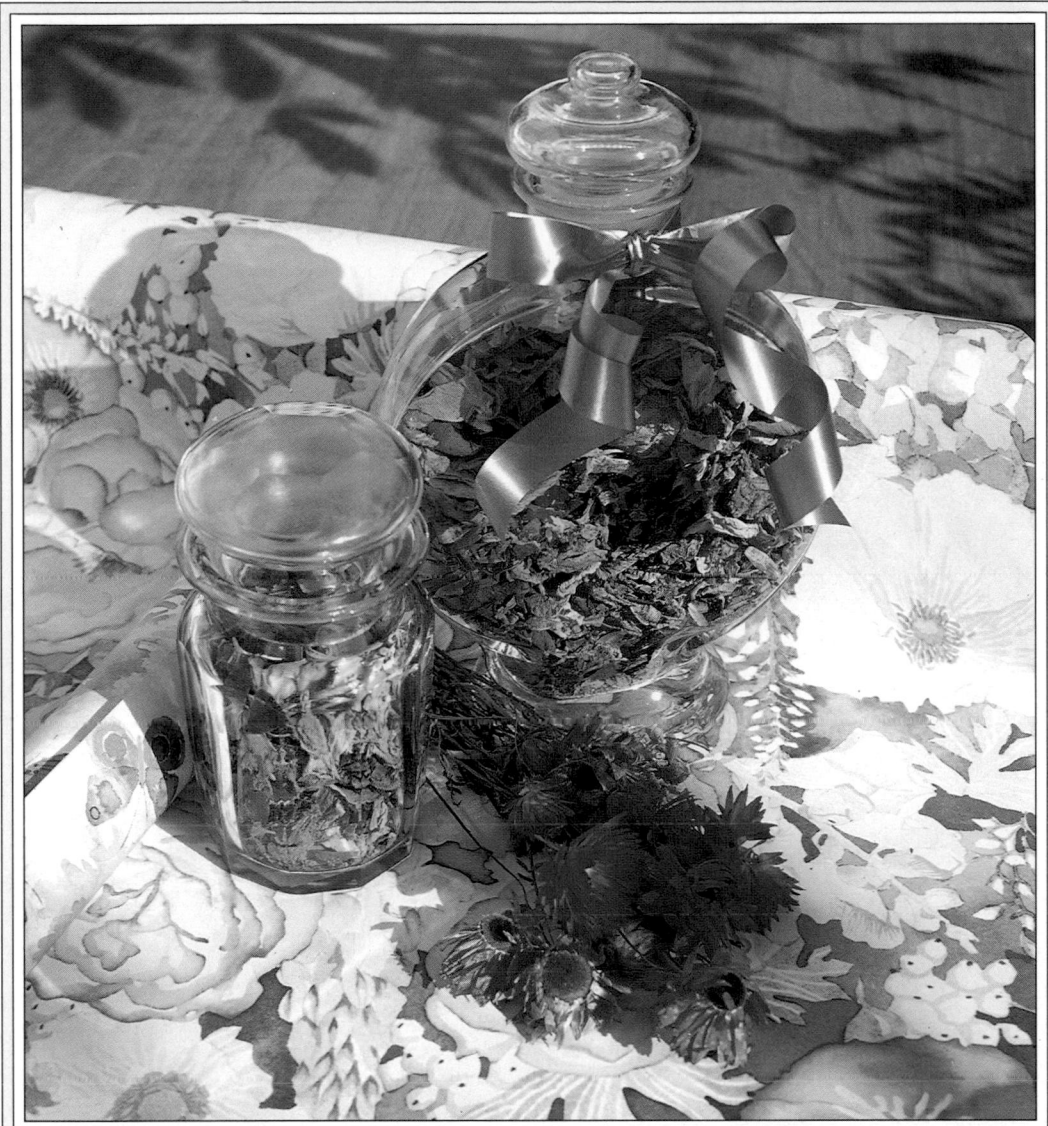

ABOVE: A traditional rose petal pot-pourri, Sweet Rose is made in a slightly unusual way using aromatic vanilla pods.

SWEET ROSE

6 cups of strong scented dried rose petals
6 dried bay leaves – finely chopped
4 dried vanilla pods
2 tbsp of coarse salt
1 tbsp of ground nutmeg
1 tbsp of orris root powder
1 tbsp of powdered cinnamon
A large screw-top jar

This pot-pourri is made by a slightly different method, even though it uses all dried ingredients. The addition of the vanilla pods gives the pot-pourri an exotic and unusual aroma.

Set aside the vanilla pods and 1 tablespoon of the coarse salt, and mix all the other ingredients together well. Place the vanilla pods round the inside edge of the jar in an upright position. Now fill the jar with layers of your mixture, sprinkling the remaining salt between each layer. Finish with a final layer of salt on top. Secure the jar tightly and leave it undisturbed for at least a month.

HERBAL DELIGHT

1 cup of dried lavender flowers
½ cup of dried mint
½ cup of dried marjoram
½ cup of dried oregano flowers
1 cup of dried lemon verbena
2 tbsp of orris root powder
3 or 4 drops of lavender essential oil

Herbs have always been renowned for their restorative and relaxing properties. The combined scents of dried herbs and lavender create a soothing mixture, ideal for a bedroom or bathroom.

Mix all the dried ingredients together in a large bowl, then add two tablespoons of orris root powder. Carefully add the lavender essential oil, one drop at a time, and mix it in thoroughly using a metal spoon.

Finally, place the mixture in an airtight container and leave it to mature for four to six weeks in a cool, dark place. Shake the mixture occasionally.

ABOVE: An aromatic and soothing pot-pourri, Herbal Delight emits a wonderfully subtle fragrance.

SANDALWOOD BOX

1 cup of whole dried yellow rose heads
1 cup of whole dried marigold heads
½ cup of mixed dried bay and
lemon verbena leaves
½ cup of mixed dried yellow petals and
flowers, such as helichrysum (strawflowers),
dahlia, or achillea
Larch cones and beech masts (nuts)
3 tbsp of orris root powder
1 tbsp of dried lemon peel (zest)

1 tbsp each of cinnamon, cloves and nutmeg
3 drops of sandalwood essential oil

An antique box or old-fashioned tea caddy makes a perfect container in which to keep and display this golden, wood-fragrant pot-pourri. Add just a few larch cones and beech masts (nuts) or whole flowerheads for a finishing touch.

Mix the petals, flowers and leaves together in a large bowl. Stir in the spices, lemon peel (zest) and orris root powder and mix well. Now add the essential oil, drop by drop, stirring it well with a metal spoon.

Put the mixture into a sealed container, and place somewhere cool and dry. Leave to mature for four to six weeks, shaking the container occasionally.

A tiny tea chest makes an ideal container for a desktop pot-pourri such as Sandalwood Box. It can be kept closed mostly, keeping the scent in, and opened when the desk is in use.

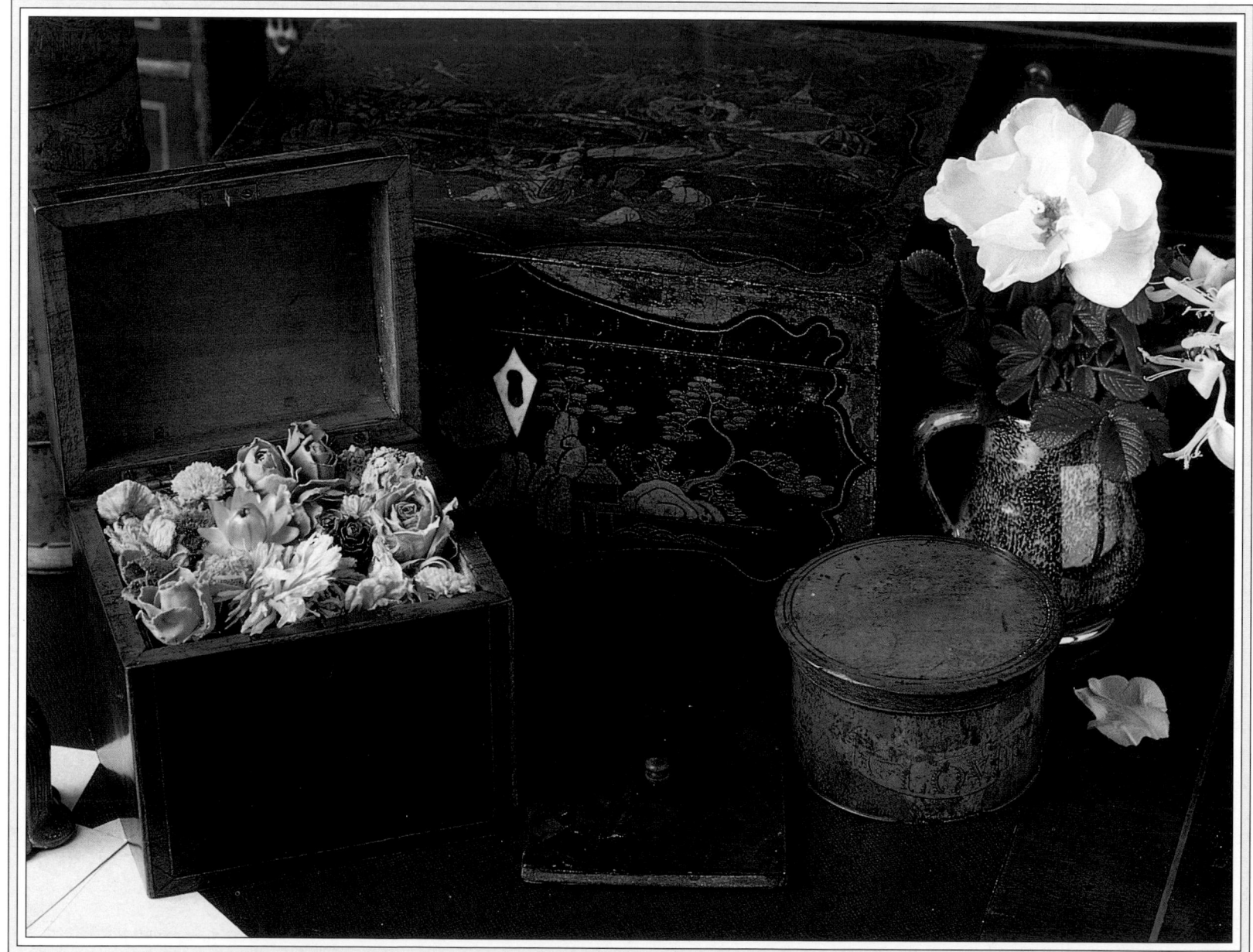

SPICE BOWL

1 cup of dried lemon verbena leaves
½ cup of dried rose petals
1 cup of whole coriander seeds
1 tbsp of allspice berries
6 whole nutmegs
1 tbsp of whole star anise
1 tbsp of crushed cinnamon bark
1 tsp each of ground nutmeg and coriander
2 tbsp of orris root powder
4 drops of cedarwood essential oil

Old storage tins designed for spices and other kitchen ingredients look good filled with a suitably spicy pot-pourri such as this one. This recipe produces a rather masculine fragrance — clean and slightly exotic.

Place the dried leaves and petals into a large bowl and stir together. Add the orris

BELOW: This Spice Bowl pot-pourri mixture is displayed in an old canister, possibly once used for storing spices.

ABOVE: This golden, spicy Marigold Mix is decorated with preserved yellow roses and cinnamon sticks.

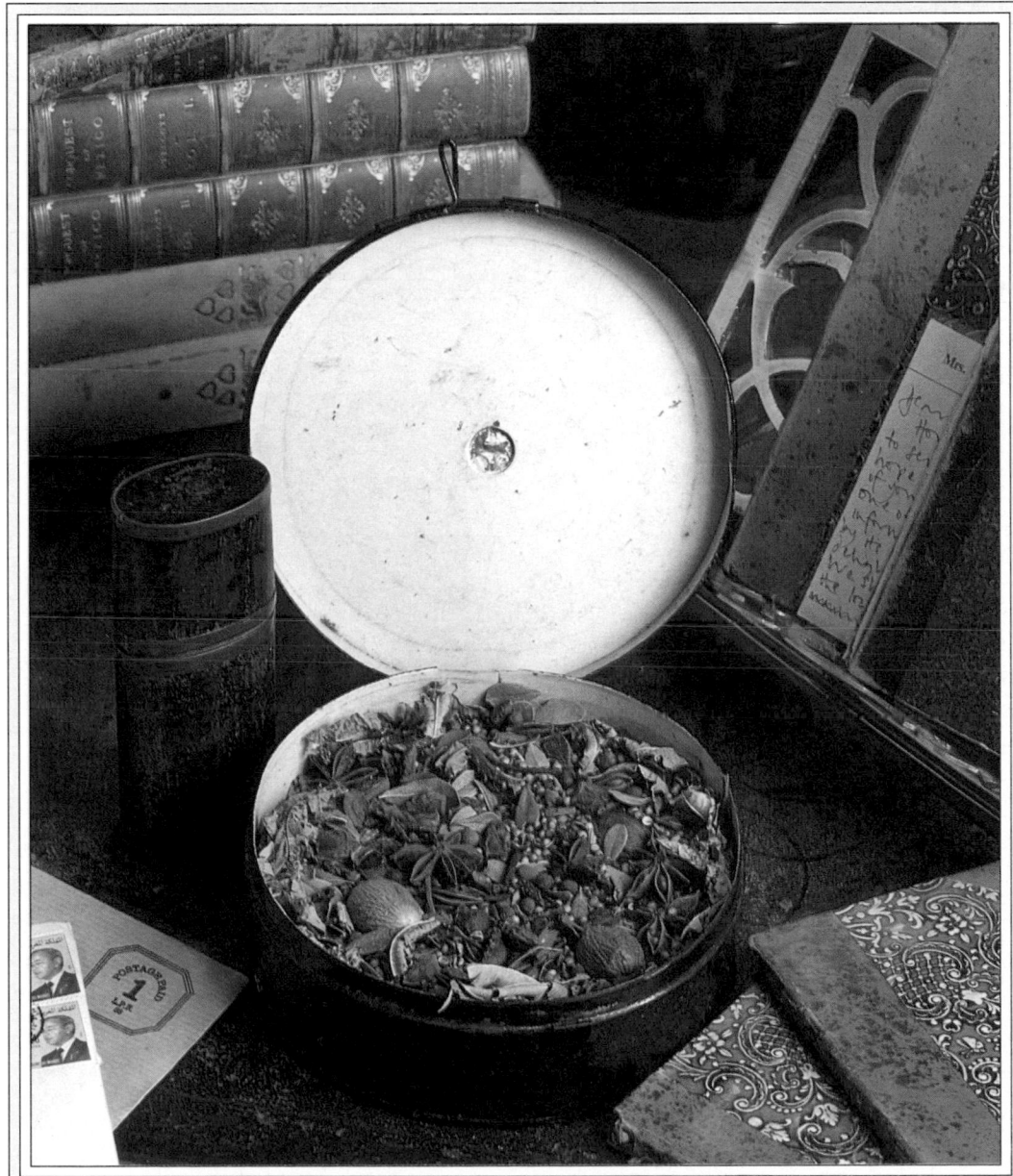

root powder and spices and mix again. Now add the drops of essential oil very carefully, mixing everything together with a metal spoon.

Put the mixture into a sealed container and leave to mature for four to six weeks, shaking the contents occasionally.

MARIGOLD MIX

1 cup of dried marigold flowers
4 or 5 yellow roseheads
4 or 5 broken cinnamon sticks
1 tbsp of cloves
1 tbsp of star anise
1 tbsp of allspice berries
2 tbsp of small eucalyptus leaves
1 tbsp of orris root powder
3 or 4 drops of cinnamon or allspice essential oil

This golden pot-pourri smells as good as it looks! You can either add a few dried yellow roseheads for the finishing touch, or use several whole marigold heads.

Place the marigolds, spices and leaves in a large bowl and mix them well with a large metal spoon. Add the orris root powder and stir the mixture thoroughly.

Carefully add the essential oil, drop by drop, stir the mixture, then place it in an airtight container for four to six weeks, shaking it occasionally.

Presenting Pot-Pourri

The different ways of displaying and using pot-pourris are endless. At first you may simply want to display your newly made pot-pourri in a large bowl, but it is worth considering other ways of presenting it.

Large containers made from wood, metal or ceramic are all suitable, enabling you to spread out the ingredients and appreciate fully the beauty of the different flowers and leaves as well as the delicious scents.

There are also many other ways of presenting your pot-pourri. Baskets lined with pretty fabric make attractive containers, especially if you tuck dried flowerheads into the rim, for example.

Boxes are another good idea. A polished wood box or a prettily papered cardboard box creates the perfect foil for a mixture of colourful petals (see page 146).

Or use an illustrated biscuit or kitchen tin. The lid can be replaced occasionally to preserve the scent of the pot-pourri.

ABOVE: An antique tea cup and saucer play the perfect host to a colourful pot-pourri.

RIGHT: Pot-pourri can be layered in glass, colour by colour, for an effective result.

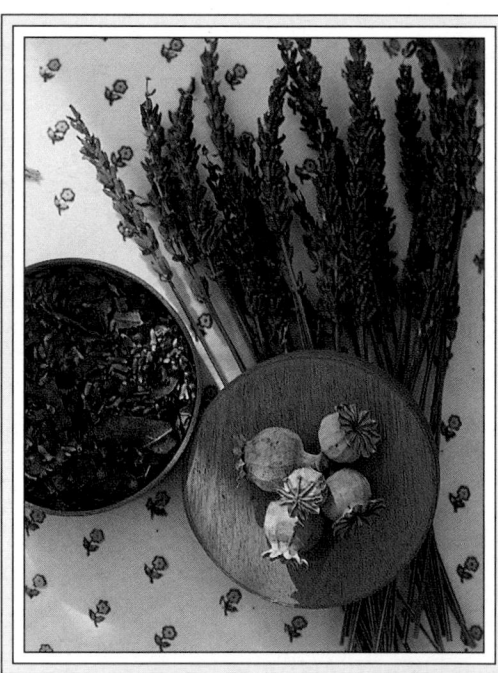

ABOVE: This simple wooden box, filled with pot-pourri, has a handful of dried poppy seedheads glued firmly to the lid for a handle and decoration all in one.

TEA PARTY

Antique china provides the perfect setting for many pot-pourris. Sugar bowls and large cups that no longer belong to a service are ideal, and they can be found quite cheaply in antique markets and junk shops.

BOXING CLEVER

Plain, undecorated wooden boxes make ideal containers for pot-pourri. They can be painted, stencilled, varnished or sprayed. A clever idea is to gather small clusters of dried flowers or seedheads and glue them on to the lid. Poppy seedheads look lovely left their natural, sculptured greyish green. Alternatively, spray them gold or silver.

GOOD IN GLASS

Clear glass is not usually very sympathetic with the texture of dried petals and leaves, but layering different coloured flowers in simple modern glass containers such as tanks and cylinders can look wonderful, particularly in a modern setting.

ABOVE: Transform an ordinary cardboard box with colourful, stripy wallpaper which echoes the petals of the pot-pourri. Alternatively, use an attractive floral wallpaper.

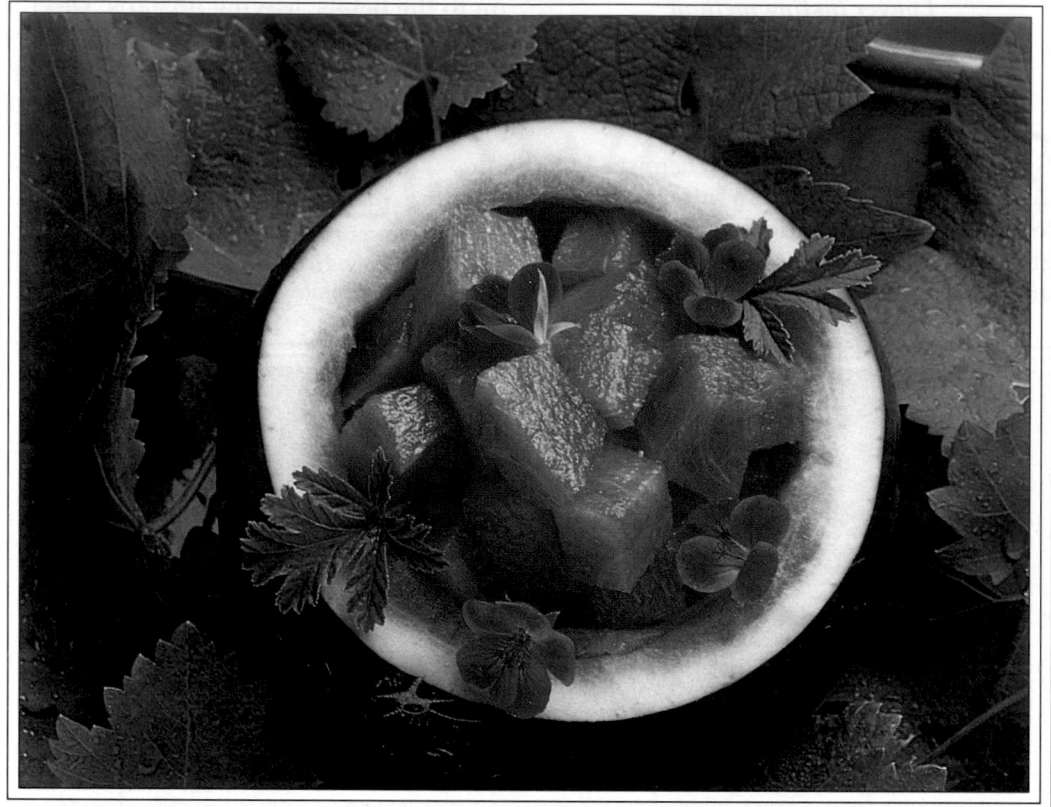

ABOVE: Water melon is infused with borage and decorated with scented geranium.

MIXED CHICORY SALAD

1 small oak leaf lettuce
1 small cos lettuce
A few leaves of frisée
1 head of Belgian chicory
1 small red radicchio
Vinaigrette
Chicory flowers

Wild chicory or succory (*Cichorium intybus*) and its commercially grown varieties — such as Belgian chicory — bears beautiful sky blue, and sometimes pink, flowers. It has a delicious bitter taste which transforms ordinary leafy salads. Another type of chicory, *Cichorium endivia*, is more commonly known as endive or frisée; it has a red cultivar called radiccio. This salad combines several chicory types.

Wash and dry the leaves of the lettuce and the various chicories. Arrange them in a salad bowl and toss with a sweetish vinaigrette. Decorate with blue chicory flowers. **Serves 6-8.**

GERANIUM MELON

Small water melon
½ pt (300ml / 1¼ cups) of water
2½ oz (75g / ⅓ cup) of caster (superfine) sugar
Juice of 1 lemon and 1 lime
Strips of lemon peel (zest)
Borage (Borago) leaves and flowers
Scented geranium flowers

This colourful combination makes a wonderfully refreshing starter or dessert.

Extract the fruit from the water melon and remove the pips. Then chop the melon into rough cubes.

Mix together the water, sugar, lemon peel and borage leaves and add the melon cubes. Simmer for a few minutes to combine the flavours, strain and allow to cool. Add the lemon and lime juice and put the mixture back into the scooped-out melon.

SUMMER SALAD

Mixed lettuce leaves
Nasturtium, cornflower and borage
(Borago) flowerheads
Dill
Dressing:
2 tbsp of olive oil
1 tbsp of walnut oil
1 tsp of made French mustard
1 tbsp of white wine vinegar
Salt and ground pepper

This attractive salad, rich in vitamin C, can be eaten as a first course or on its own.

The flowers should be fresh, unblemished and unsprayed. If possible, do not wash them, as the petals bruise easily. Check for insects and pick the flowerheads off the stems. Mix the nasturtiums and other flowers with the lettuce leaves.

To make the dressing, put all the ingredients together in a screw-top jar and shake vigorously. Carefully toss the dressing with the salad just before serving.

ABOVE: Nasturtiums are among the easiest perennials to grow. Eaten when freshly picked, they make a dazzling Summer Salad.

RIGHT: Chicory adds a bitterness to salads which enlivens the taste dramatically. The blue flowers provide an attractive contrast.

RIGHT: Aromatic thyme lends a wonderful flavour to grilled chicken. The flowering sprigs create the perfect decoration.

CHICKEN AND THYME

4 skinned chicken breasts
Long stems of thyme in bloom
Bunch of fresh thyme leaves
3 tbsp of corn oil
Juice of 2 lemons
Salt and pepper

Chicken cooked with thyme tastes absolutely delicious and this appetizing dish is the perfect choice for an informal summer lunch or barbecue party.

Chop or grind the bunch of thyme and mix in a large bowl with the oil, lemon juice and seasoning. Add the chicken pieces to the mixture and leave to marinate for two hours, turning the chicken occasionally.

Remove the chicken just before cooking and allow it to drain, but make sure that you leave plenty of the chopped thyme on the chicken pieces.

Cook the chicken over a medium hot barbecue for approximately 20 minutes. For extra flavour, dip the flowering thyme into the marinade and lay it over the chicken while the underside is cooking. Reserve some for decoration.
Serves 4.

MARIGOLD FILLETS

4 fillets of smoked mackerel or herring
Small green lettuce
Sauce:
2 tbsp of sunflower oil
4 tbsp of cider vinegar
2 heaped tsp of grated horseradish
8 marigold (Calendula officinalis) flowerheads

Serve succulent smoked mackerel or herring fillets on a bed of orange marigold flowers and crisp green lettuce for a winning summer party dish.

Pour the vinegar into a mixing bowl, add the horseradish and crush well with a wooden spoon. Blend in the sunflower oil and leave to infuse for 30 minutes.

Wash the flowers and drain well. Cut the fish fillets in half lengthways and arrange in a star shape on a bed of lettuce.

Finally, stir the marigold petals into the sauce and spoon some of it over the dish. Reserve the remainder to serve separately.
Serves 4.

ABOVE: Bright green lettuce and orange marigolds frame a star of smoked fish fillets.

MARIGOLD MUSTARD

2 tbsp of dried marigold (Calendula officinalis) flowers
8oz (225g) pot of strong, grainy mustard

This unusual mustard is excellent served with cold pork or ham.

Finely chop the marigolds and put them into a mixing bowl. Add the whole jar of mustard and mix thoroughly, making sure that the flowers are well distributed.

Spoon the mustard into a suitable container (you can wash the original mustard container and soak off the label if it's an attractive jar). Seal the jar and add a label or little yellow ribbon if you wish.

RIGHT: This recipe uses spicy marigold petals to jazz up a plain, grainy mustard.

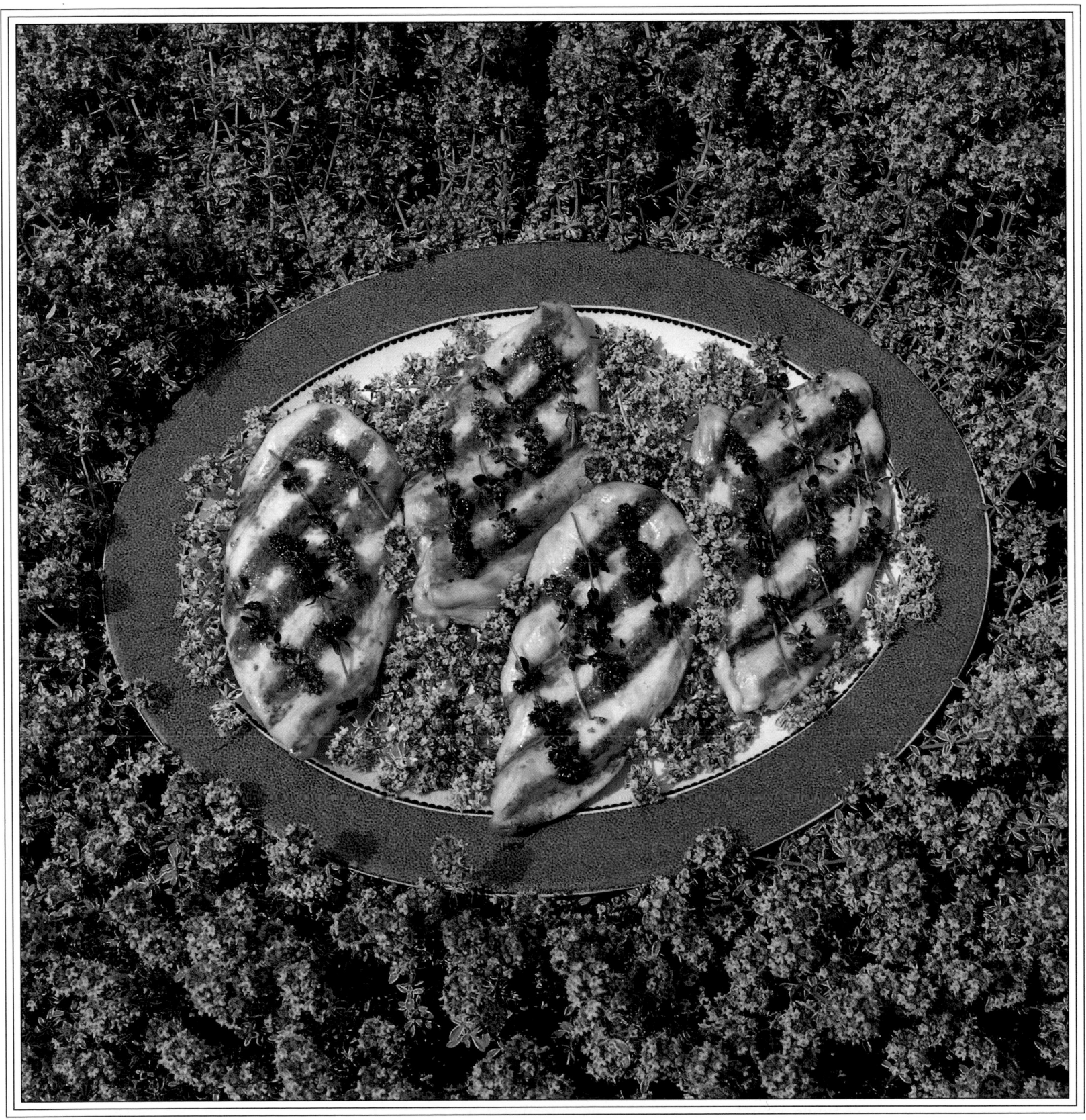

NECTARINE AND BORAGE SALAD

4 nectarines
Juice of half a lemon or lime
Fresh borage (Borago) flowers

At the height of summer, when fruit is at its best and most plentiful, make a simple fruit salad with borage.

Wash the nectarines and slice them into thin segments. They look best with the deep red skin left on the orange flesh.

Layer the nectarine slices in a deep bowl, adding a sprinkling of lime or lemon juice. Scatter the borage flowers over the fruit and serve immediately. Peaches can be substituted for nectarines.
Serves 4.

ELDERFLOWER CHEESECAKE

8oz (250g / 2 cups) of crushed digestive
biscuits (Graham crackers)
2oz (50g / ¼ cup) of melted butter
8oz (250g / 1 cup) of cream cheese
2 eggs, separated
4 tbsp of Greek set yoghurt
2 tbsp of honey
Handful of chopped elderflowers
2oz (50g / ½ cup) of sultanas (golden
raisins) soaked overnight in
3 tbsp of elderflower wine
4fl oz (100ml / scant ½ cup) of thick cream

Elderflowers add a tasty tang to this delicious cheesecake. First, mix the crushed biscuits with the melted butter, and press the mixture into the base of an 8in (20cm) loose-bottomed baking tin.

Beat the butter and honey together, then beat in the egg yolks. Next mix in the cream cheese, the wine and sultanas. Beat the egg whites until stiff and fold into the mixture. Pour into the biscuit-lined baking tin and cook in a moderate oven for 40 minutes. Set aside to cool.

To decorate, whip the thick cream until it is stiff, adding a little sugar to taste if you like. Put the cream into a piping bag (pastry bag) and, using a fluted nozzle, pipe cream around the edge of the cheesecake.

This simple dish of sliced nectarines is liberally sprinkled with edible, star-shaped borage flowers.

ABOVE: A traditional baked cheesecake is enlivened with tangy elderflower.

STUFFED NASTURTIUMS

2oz (50g / ¼ cup) of granulated sugar
6oz (175g / ¾ cup) of ricotta cheese
1 drop of pure almond essence
4oz (100g / ⅔ cup) of blanched almonds, finely chopped
4fl oz (100ml / scant ½ cup) of thick cream, stiffly whipped
16 nasturtium flowers

This recipe makes a pretty and delicious summer pudding.

Gather the flowers when they are fresh and have just fully opened. Avoid washing them if possible, but do ensure that they are unblemished and are free from pesticides and insects.

Lightly beat the sugar into the cheese and when the sugar has dissolved add the almond essence to the mixture. Toast the chopped almonds in a hot oven, watching carefully so they do not burn. Remove, and leave them to cool.

Fold the whipped cream into the cheese mixture and add the toasted almonds to it. Then taste and adjust the sweetening and the flavouring. Take small spoonfuls of the mixture and stuff each flower. Serve with a colourful fresh fruit salad or a fruit sauce. ***Serves 4.***

BELOW: Offer guests this tasty pudding made from nasturtium flowers filled with cream cheese and crunchy toasted almonds.

VIOLET SPONGE

4 eggs
4oz (125g / 1 cup) of self-raising
(all-purpose) flour
4oz (125g / ½ cup) of sugar
1oz (25g / 1 tbsp) of melted butter
8fl oz (25ml / 1 cup) of thick cream
2 tbsp of violet liqueur (see page 117)
Bunch of violets

Violets add a subtle fragrance and a delicate taste to this traditional sponge cake. First, brush two 7in (18cm) baking tins with oil and line the base of the tins with oiled greaseproof paper.

Place a bowl containing the eggs and sugar over a pan of hot water and, using an electric whisk, beat fast until the mixture becomes thick and fluffy, and will hold the impression of the whisk. Sift in a quarter of the flour and fold in with a metal spoon. Gradually fold in the remainder of the flour, and lastly the cooled melted butter.

Immediately turn the mixture out into the baking tins and bake in a fairly hot oven (190°C/375°F/gas mark 5) for about 30 minutes. Turn out on to a wire rack to cool. When cold drizzle violet liqueur over each sponge base.

BELOW: This fabulous sponge cake is made in the traditional way and drizzled with a little delicious violet liqueur. The rich, deep purple of the fresh violets are the perfect decoration.

For the filling, beat the cream and reserve two tablespoons for piping. Spread the remaining cream over one of the sponges and place the other sponge on top.

Pipe rosettes of cream around the edge of the filling and make a garland of rosettes on the top of the cake.

Finally, carefully wash and dry the violets, and cut away the bracts. Push the flowers into the cream around the filling and pile the remaining violets in the centre of the cream garland.

MARIGOLD CAKE

8oz (250g / 1 cup) of softened butter
8oz (250g / 1 cup) of caster (superfine) sugar
4 eggs, beaten
8oz (250g / 2 cups) of self-raising
(all-purpose) flour
Grated rind (zest) of 1 orange and 1 lemon
3 tbsp of fresh marigold (Calendula officinalis) petals or 2 tbsp of dried
Granulated sugar (optional)

Marigold petals give a delicate flavour and a slight orange hue to this deliciously light tea-time cake.

First, grease and line a 2lb (1kg) loaf tin. Cream the butter together with the sugar and add the beaten egg a little at a time. Sieve the flour with the baking powder and fold into the creamed mixture. Stir in the orange and lemon rinds and the petals.

Spoon the mixture into the tin and bake in a preheated oven 350°F (180°C or gas mark 4) for about 1 hour. Sprinkle with granulated sugar about halfway through the cooking time if desired. Cool for 5 minutes, then remove from the tin. Serve when just cool.
Serves 8/10

RIGHT: This delicious cake is made from a traditional sponge recipe with fresh marigold petals added to give a subtle flavour.

ABOVE: Capture summer scents and flavours with this delicious lemon-geranium and apple preserve.

GERANIUM PRESERVE

*4lb (2kg) of cooking apples
1¾ pt (1 litre) of water
Granulated or preserving sugar
Juice of 2 lemons
15 scented geranium leaves*

Scented geraniums are wonderfully old-fashioned plants. Their leaves smell of rose, lemon, eucalyptus, ginger, lime, balsam and orange. The lemon- or rose-scented leaves make the most delicious preserves.

Chop the apples roughly, leaving the skin, stalks and pips. Put in a large pan with the water and simmer until soft. Strain for several hours through a jelly bag or muslin; do not squeeze the fruit pulp through or the preserve will be cloudy.

Measure the juice into a preserving pan and for every pint (600ml) of juice add 1lb (450g) of sugar. Add the lemon juice and the geranium leaves. Stir over a low heat, then boil rapidly until set, for about 10 minutes. Quickly remove the leaves and pour into clean, warm jars. Cover while still hot.

Serve with home-made bread or plain scones. Alternatively, use as a filling for a sponge cake, reserving some leaves and petals for decoration.

ROSE HIP JELLY

*1lb (450g) of cooking apples, unpeeled and quartered
2lb (900g) of rose hips, roughly chopped
2pt (1 litre) of water
Juice of 1 lemon
Granulated sugar*

Rose hips are ripe from late summer to autumn and can be preserved in this lovely jelly. The result is sharp and fruity with a beautiful garnet colour.

Put the apples and rose hips into a large saucepan and pour over the water to just cover. Boil gently for about 1 hour, until the fruit is very soft.

Pour into a jelly bag or a square of muslin and hang up to drip over a large bowl. Do not press the fruit pulp or the jelly will be cloudy. Leave overnight.

The next day, measure out the drained juice and, for every pint (600ml) of juice, measure 1lb (450g) of sugar. Put the juice and sugar into a saucepan and heat slowly until the sugar has dissolved. Now, boil rapidly for about 10 minutes until a setting point is reached.

Skim any foam from the surface and pour into hot, sterilized jars. When cool, seal the jars in the usual way. This jelly is delicious served with roast lamb or game.
Makes about 1½-2lb (700-900g)

ABOVE: Rose hip jelly has a wonderful garnet glow. It tastes fruity and sharp.

BELOW: This golden honey is delicately flavoured with lavender.

LAVENDER HONEY

Small jar of runny honey
Handful of fresh lavender flowers
Small bunch of lavender to decorate

This delicately flavoured honey is so easy to prepare and makes an attractive gift.

Warm the honey and lavender flowers in a heatproof bowl over a saucepan of simmering water for about 15 minutes. Do not allow the honey to boil.

Strain the honey through a fine sieve and discard the lavender flowers. Pour into a sterilized jar and, when cool, seal. Decorate the jar with a sprig of lavender flowers and a little pale mauve ribbon.

ROSE PETAL JELLY

4lb (2kg) of cooking apples
2pts (1 litre) of water
Juice of 2 lemons
Granulated or preserving sugar
1pt (600ml) scented rose petals

Rose petals make a delicious, sweet jelly. However, by themselves they can be rather cloying, so it is best to make a sharp-flavoured base from apples or redcurrants.

Chop the apples, leaving the skin stalks and pips. Put in a large pan with the water and simmer until soft. Put into a jelly bag and strain for several hours (don't squeeze the pulp as this will make the jelly cloudy).

Measure the juice into a preserving pan and for every pint (600ml) of juice add 1lb (450g) of sugar. Add the lemon juice and rose petals. Stir over a low heat to dissolve the sugar then boil rapidly for about 10 minutes until it sets. Remove the petals and pour the jelly into clean, warm jars. Cover while still hot and label.
Makes about 4lb/2kg

RIGHT: Rose petal jelly turns plain bread and scones into a special tea-time treat.

CLARET PUNCH

1 tbsp of caster (superfine) sugar
8oz (250g) of fresh strawberries
Small strips of cucumber peel
Juice of 3 lemons
3 tbsp of brandy
2 tbsp of Cointreau or orange liqueur
2 bottles of claret or similar red wine

1 bottle of sparkling mineral water,
soda or lemonade
Borage (Borago) flowers and mint

This delicious cherry-red wine cup is best served from a clear glass bowl to appreciate the sparkling colour and pretty decoration. Dissolve the sugar in a little hot water and pour into a large bowl. Slice the strawber-ries if they are large and add to the bowl together with the cucumber strips, lemon juice, brandy and Cointreau. Pour in the red wine and top up with the sparkling water, soda or lemonade. Chill well.

When the punch is ready to serve, add ice and decorate it with a liberal sprinkling of borage flowers and mint sprigs.
Serves 20.

VIOLET LIQUEUR

18fl oz (500ml / 2 cups) of vodka
50 heads of scented Parma violets
7oz (200g / ¾ cup) white sugar
¼ in (5mm) strip of vanilla bean

Otherwise known as parfait-amour, this sweet violet liqueur makes a delicious after-dinner drink. Its deep purple colour and heady aroma put it in a class of its own.

Put all the ingredients in a jar and leave for several weeks, shaking occasionally. When ready, strain through muslin, then again through a coffee filter paper, until clear. For an even prettier effect, you can add a few drops of purple food colouring.
Makes 1pt (600ml)

FLORAL ICE CUBES

Suitable flowers include : rose petals, tiny sprigs of mint or thyme in flower, scented geranium blooms, primroses, violets, borage (Borago) and lavender.
Ice tray and water

Flowers or petals encapsulated in cubes of ice look wonderfully pretty floating in summer drinks or used as table decorations. Float them in bowls of wine cup or pile them around a glass serving dish filled with a cool, creamy, summer pudding.

Put a flower in each ice-tray section. Half fill with water and freeze. Top up with

BELOW: Rich, heady violet liqueur is not surprisingly known as 'perfect love'.

water and freeze again. Freezing like this means the flower is in the middle of the ice, as it tends to float to the top of the water.

LEFT: Decorated with borage and fresh mint, this cooling claret cup is based on a 19th-century recipe.

BELOW: Edible flowers encased in ice make enchanting and unusual decorations for special summer drinks.

APPLE-MINT LEMONADE

4 lemons
3½ oz (100g / ½ cup) of caster
(superfine) sugar
1¼ pt (750ml / 2¾ cups) of water
Apple mint and/or lemon balm sprigs
Mint flowers and sprigs to decorate

Home-made lemonade is easy to make and this version has the refreshing taste of apple mint as a bonus. If you intend to store the lemonade for long, it's best to remove the lemon rind (zest) from the fruit first, as it can give the drink a bitter taste.

Scrub the lemons thoroughly to remove any wax or residual spray. Peel strips thin-

Home-made lemonade is enhanced by adding lemon balm or apple mint.

ly from the skin and put them into a heat-proof jug. Add the sugar and pour over just enough boiling water to dissolve it. Finally, add the sprigs of mint and leave to cool.

Squeeze the juice from the lemons into the syrup. Remove the mint, but leave the lemon peel. Top up with cold water according to taste.

When ready to serve, add plenty of ice and slices of freshly cut lemon. Decorate with a couple of sprigs of fresh mint — flowering mint looks particularly attractive when in season.

ROSE AND VANILLA TEA BAGS

2 cups of dried scented rose petals
6 dried rose hips
Dried rind (zest) of 1 orange
1 vanilla pod
Nappy (diaper) liners
Cotton twist thread

The subtle combination of aromatic vanilla and scented rose makes a refreshing drink. You can either drink it hot or chilled for a sensational summer drink.

Carefully strip the peel off the rose hips and chop it up. Then add a finely chopped vanilla pod and the dried rind (zest) of the orange peel. Cut the rose petals into very small pieces and add to the mixture. Stir well with a metal spoon.

Cut each nappy (diaper) liner into four circles. Place two teaspoons of the mixture

BELOW: Rose and vanilla tea bags make a refreshing drink, either hot or cold.

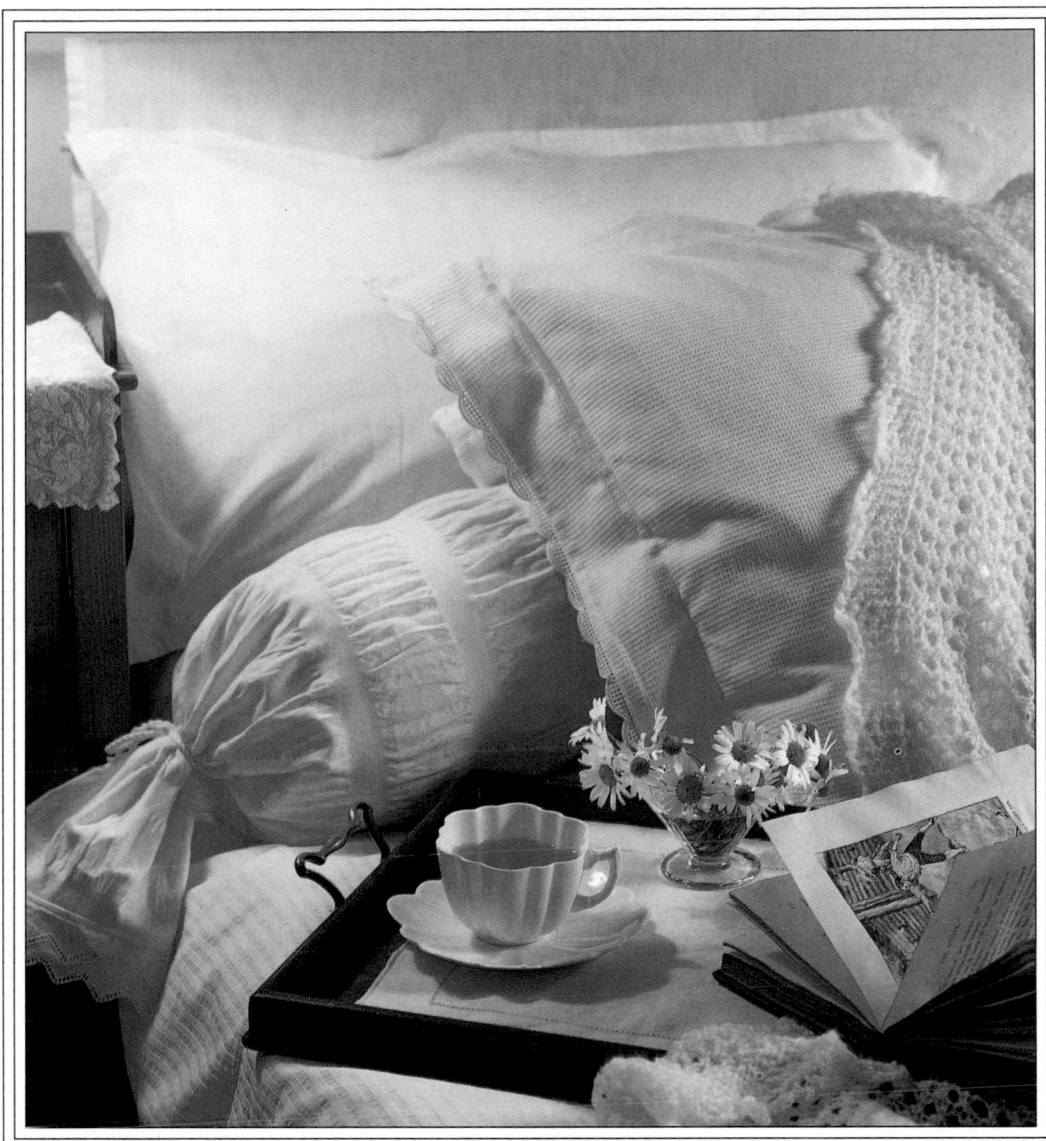

ABOVE: Chamomile tisane is easily made by infusing a spoonful of dried flowers in a teapot of boiling water. After a few minutes the tisane can be strained before drinking.

in the centre of each circle. Bring the edges to the centre and tie tightly with cotton twist, leaving one long end for ease of handling. Trim the surplus from the top of the liner, and store in an airtight tin.

When making the tea, allow one bag per cup. Pour boiling water on to the bag and leave to steep for five minutes. If desired, you can sweeten the tea with honey.

TISANES

As well as adding scent and flavour to conventional teas, flowers can be used to make tisanes. Use 1 teaspoon of dried flowers or 3 teaspoons of fresh per cup, and steep them in boiling water for about 3 or 4 minutes before drinking. Make in a jug and strain into a cup. Add a slice of lemon and sweeten with honey if desired.

You can also add flowers to ordinary loose tea by adding roughly 2 tablespoons of either strongly scented rose petals, jasmine, marigold or lime flowers to 6 tablespoons of tea leaves.

FLOWERS FOR BEAUTY

Small muslin bags filled with flowers and herbs scent bath water in a natural way.

We never seem to grow tired of flower scents in the beauty preparations we use. And nowadays, more than ever before, we feel the need for simple and straightforward products that are as far removed as possible from the chemist's laboratory. This chapter is packed with ideas for making your own preparations from a wide range of pure, natural ingredients.

There is a long tradition of using flowers for beauty. In addition to their usefulness as medicines, flowers, leaves and herbs were long ago discovered to have all kinds of therapeutic and beneficial qualities when they were steeped in various lotions and creams, or simply used as an infusion.

Throughout the centuries, flowers were found to contain qualities that soothed and softened skin, brightened and strengthened hair, or simply relaxed and scented a tired body in a deliciously fragrant bath.

The rose has a long association with beauty. Its irresistible fragrance makes it a popular choice for perfuming all kinds of beauty products, from shampoo to hand cream.

There are many recipes that you can make at home. You could start with a simple infusion of flowers to use as a foot bath or facial, or try some scented bath bags.

The recipes in this chapter are made with pure, natural ingredients. Be aware, however, that the properties of some plants are stronger than others and, although it is extremely unlikely, there is the possibility that some ingredients may irritate sensitive skin. If you are sensitive to certain plants, you can always adapt and alter a recipe to suit your taste.

STERILIZING BOTTLES AND JARS

To keep all your recipes free from possible contamination, it is best to sterilize all the bottles or jars that you intend to use.

The oldest method of sterilization is to boil the item but today this is not the best method, particularly if you are using delicate glass. Instead, try one of the sterilizing products on the market, which are either for use with babies' feeding bottles or for home wine making. Simply follow the manufacturer's instructions.

REFRIGERATION

Many home-made creams and lotions benefit from being kept in the refrigerator. As the recipes involve natural products, they are unlikely to last as long as commercial preparations. Keeping them cold will not only preserve them longer, it will also help to improve the efficacy of some preparations — toners, for example, feel great when applied icy cold.

MAKING SACHETS

Bath sachets are easily made from muslin, cheesecloth or any gauzy fabric through which the ingredients can infuse.

They are nothing more than strips of fabric about 13in by 3in (33cm by 8cm) which are folded in half and sewn up both sides. Once they have been turned the right way and filled with the ingredients, the top edge can be pinked or neatly hemmed and tied with pretty ribbon or string.

If sewing doesn't appeal to you, you can make a bath bag very easily without having to pick up a needle. Simply cut a square or circle of fabric and put a spoonful of your chosen mixture in the middle. Gather up the edges and tie the sachet securely with string, ribbon or thread.

ROSE PETAL WATER

5 cups of fresh, strongly scented, rose petals
Bottled mineral water
Vodka or
pure medicinal alcohol

Home-made rose petal water is lovely to use as a mild skin toner and freshener. It is gentle and sweetly fragrant and you can

This lovely fragrant Rose Petal Water is ideal as a gentle, fragrant skin tonic.

also use it to sprinkle in your bath water.

Put the rose petals into a large bowl and heat up the mineral water. When the water has reached boiling point, pour it over the rose petals.

When cool, mix in the vodka. Do not buy good quality spirit — cheap vodka works just as well. You will need one part vodka to 10 parts water. Leave to infuse.

When cold, strain the rose-petal liquid into sterilized bottles. A petal or two added to the bottle before sealing adds a decorative touch. Cap the bottle securely with a cork or tight stopper.

ROSE LOTION

2 cups of deep red rose petals, fresh or dried
1 cup of bottled mineral water
1 cup of white wine vinegar
½ cup of bought rosewater

This is an alternative recipe to the Rose Petal Water that doesn't use alcohol.

Put the petals in a screw-top jar. Boil the water and vinegar and pour on the petals. Leave for several days, shaking it daily. Then, add the rosewater, shake well and decant into a sterilized, stoppered bottle.

POPPY AND CORNFLOWER LOTION

2 tbsp of dried poppy petals
1 tbsp of dried cornflowers
½ pt (300ml) of bottled mineral water

This recipe is a mild facial skin toner. If you keep it in the refrigerator it will feel especially invigorating and refreshing when you apply it to your skin.

BELOW: This alcohol-free Rose Lotion makes a wonderful skin tonic.

RIGHT: A mildly astringent toner, Poppy and Cornflower Lotion lasts well when kept in the refrigerator.

Put the poppy petals and cornflowers into a small saucepan and then add the bottled water. Bring the mixture to the boil and turn off the heat. Allow the petals to infuse for at least 30-40 minutes.

When the solution is ready and has completely cooled, strain it through a fine sieve into a jug. Finally, pour it into sterilized glass bottles and seal with a cork.

ROSE PETAL FACIAL STEAM

1¾ pt (1 litre) of bottled mineral water
5 tbsp of fresh, strongly scented rose petals
2-3 drops of rose essential oil

A facial steam is a wonderful relaxant and helps open up pores to rid the skin of blackheads and other horrors.

Heat the water to boiling. Put the petals in a large bowl and pour the water over them. Add the essential oil, stir well and leave to infuse for 3 minutes.

To use the facial steam, hold your face over the bowl, but make sure you don't get too close to the water as the skin on your face is very delicate and you could cause broken veins. Drape a towel over your head to enclose the steam. Try to remain over the steam for about 10 minutes if you can, but take a breather every now and then. Finish off by dousing your skin with lukewarm water and a splash of facial tonic such as rose petal water (see page 122).

Herbs, like peppermint, sage and rosemary can all be added to the water to give a more astringent facial.

ABOVE: Made with floral essential oils and pure soap, these Geranium Soap Balls are kind to most skin types.

LEFT: Pure luxury and ten minutes' enforced rest come with this sweetly scented Rose Petal Facial Steam.

GERANIUM SOAP BALLS

1 large bar of unscented white soap
2fl oz (55ml) of bought rosewater
2 drops of grapefruit essential oil
2 drops of rose geranium essential oil
Lemon food colouring (optional)

These scented guest soaps make a lovely gift when they are wrapped in cellophane and tied with a pretty posy of dried flowers or leaves.

First grate the soap into a bowl. Then gently heat the rosewater in a heatproof bowl over a pan of simmering water. Pour the rosewater over the grated soap and stir.

To this softened mixture carefully add the essential oils, drop by drop, and mix thoroughly with a metal spoon. If you want to colour the soap, now is the time to add the lemon food colouring. When the soap is well blended, let it stand for one or two days. Then break it into small pieces and roll each one into a ball.

Polish the soap balls with cotton wool (absorbent cotton) dipped in a little rosewater or almond oil.

ABOVE: Pretty pink Carnation and Clove Soaps welcome guests to the washroom. They also make ideal gifts.

CARNATION AND CLOVE SOAP

10oz (300g) of plain, unscented soap
9fl oz (250ml) of water
4 drops of pink food colouring
5 drops of carnation essential oil
1 drop of clove essential oil

A lovely gift idea, but you might prefer to keep these pretty soaps for yourself!

Grate the soap into a mixing bowl. Boil the water and pour it over the soap. Add the food colouring and stir well.

Take the essential oils and add them to the mixture, drop by drop. Mix the ingredients thoroughly with a metal spoon and leave the mixture to harden.

When the soap has hardened, break off small pieces and mould them into smallish balls. When they are really hard, polish each ball of soap with a little cotton wool (absorbent cotton) dipped into almond oil.

BATH BAG

1 cup of wheat bran
1 cup of oatmeal
½ cup of dried milk powder
1 cup of dried, highly scented rose petals
1 cup of dried lavender flowers
½ cup of dried lemon verbena leaves
or rosemary

These simple bath sachets can be hung from the running hot water tap or placed into the bath itself. The bran, oatmeal and milk act as water softeners. The other ingredients are for fragrance and can be adapted to suit personal preferences.

Mix all the ingredients together in a large bowl, then spoon the mixture into sachets (instructions for making these appear on page 121). Any surplus mixture can be stored in a screw-top jar.

ROSE GERANIUM BUBBLE BATH

5fl oz (150ml) of pure organic washing-up
(dish-washing) liquid
5fl oz (150ml) of still bottled mineral water
1 tsp of rose geranium essential oil
3 drops of pink food colouring

A fun and foaming bubble bath in a pretty pink makes a lovely gift either for yourself or for a friend.

In a small jug mix the washing-up liquid with the mineral water. Add the essential oil and stir well. To this solution add the food colouring and stir well once more.

Decant the mixture into a pretty bottle which can be decorated with some ribbon

BELOW: Bath bags may be dropped straight into the water or tied to a bath tap.

ABOVE: Rose Geranium Bubble Bath makes a lovely gift, but you can mix some just for yourself!

or a few silk flowers. Add one tablespoon of bubble bath to hot running water for a fragrant and luxurious bath.

ROSE BATH OIL

3 tbsp of glycerine
1 tbsp of rose essential oil

Bath oils help to make a relaxing experience even more pleasurable. The beauty of this bath oil is that it doesn't rely on artificial fragrances or colours, and it will help condition your skin as well.

Simply mix the glycerine well with the essential oil using a metal spooon.

Keep bottled and use only one teaspoon per bath, pouring it into the stream of running hot water.

RIGHT: A bath scented with roses is both luxurious and relaxing.

CHAMOMILE HAIR RINSE

*4 tbsp of fresh chamomile flowerheads or
2 tbsp of dried
18fl oz (500ml) of bottled mineral water
2 tbsp of distilled vinegar*

Hair rinses can be infused with many different herbs and flowers according to your hair type and colour.

Chamomile has long been used for its slight lightening qualities on blond hair, but for brown hair, substitute sage, rosemary or marigold for a darker sheen (see recipe for Rosemary and Lavender Hair Rinse below).

To make this rinse, first boil the water in a pan and add the chamomile. Take the pan off the heat and leave to infuse, then add the vinegar and allow to cool. Strain and store the mixture in sterilized bottles.

The hair rinse should be used after shampooing as follows: mix six tablespoons of rinse with 1 pint (500 ml) of warm water and pour over your hair. Towel dry and style your hair as usual.

ROSEMARY AND LAVENDER HAIR RINSE

*1 tbsp of dried lavender flowers
1 tbsp of dried rosemary
½ pt (300ml) of water
1pt (600ml) of bottled mineral water
1 tsp of lemon juice or good wine vinegar*

This rinse is excellent for dark hair. (For instructions on how to use, see recipe for Chamomile Hair Rinse above).

Pour the ordinary water into a saucepan and add the lavender flowers and rosemary. Gently bring the water to the boil. Take off the heat and allow to infuse for several hours. Strain off the liquid and add it to the bottled mineral water. Add the lemon juice or wine vinegar and pour the mixture into sterilized bottles.

LEFT: Used regularly, Chamomile Hair Rinse is said to lighten fair hair and add shine.

ELDERBERRY HAIR RINSE

4oz (115g) of fresh elderberries
(Sambucus nigra)
1pt (½ litre) of water

This is a simple recipe for those with grey hair. Use it as a final rinse to impart a slight blue/grey tint to the hair.

Put the elderberries into a bowl and crush them slightly. Bring the water to the boil and pour it over the berries. Then stir the mixture and leave it to infuse for approximately two hours.

When ready, strain the liquid into a sterilized bottle. Use the rinse as instructed in the Chamomile Hair Rinse recipe on the previous page.

It is worth looking out for pretty bottles you can use to store rinses such as this. Flea markets and bric-a-brac stalls often sell old bottles quite cheaply.

An attractive assortment of pretty bottles holds a fragrant range of floral waters (see recipes on pages 122-123) and hair rinses.

ROSE HAND CREAM

2 tbsp of fresh rose petals
4 tbsp of almond oil
8 tbsp of lanolin
4 tbsp of glycerine
4 or 5 drops of rose essential oil

Use this soothing lotion to condition hands, feet or elbows.

First, cover the rose petals with a little boiling water and leave to cool. Then gently melt the almond oil, lanolin and glycerine in a bowl over a saucepan of hot water.

Put the almond oil mixture, well-drained rose petals and rose oil into a food processor and blend thoroughly.

Finally, pour the hand cream into small sterilized glass jars with tight-fitting lids.

LEFT: A rich Rose Hand Cream can easily be made from natural ingredients.

BELOW: A beautiful shade of lemony orange, this Orange and Carrot Moisturiser uses natural carrot juice and essential oil.

ORANGE AND CARROT MOISTURISER

1 tsp of beeswax
1 tbsp of lanolin
6 tbsp of almond oil
3 tbsp of bottled mineral water
4 tbsp of carrot juice
½ tsp of borax
2 tbsp of glycerine
3 drops of sweet orange essential oil

This scented moisturiser helps protect your skin from everyday wear and tear.

Melt the beeswax with the lanolin and almond oil in a bowl set over a saucepan of simmering water. Stir gently until the ingredients have melted.

In another small saucepan, heat the water and carrot juice and dissolve the borax.

Then add the glycerine to the beeswax mixture and stir well. Remove the bowl from the saucepan and slowly add the carrot juice mixture to the beeswax mixture, whisking thoroughly until the ingredients have cooled down.

Add the essential oil and mix well. Put into a clean jar with a tight fitting lid and store in a cool place or the refrigerator.

Orange Flower Night Cream is a nourishing blend of natural oils, wax and lanolin.

ORANGE FLOWER NIGHT CREAM

2 tsp of lanolin
2 tsp of beeswax
4 tsp of almond oil
3 tsp of bottled mineral water
Pinch of borax
4 capsules of wheatgerm oil
3 or 4 drops of neroli (orange blossom) essential oil

Scented with sweet orange blossom, this is a wonderfully rich and nourishing cream that is ideal for smoothing and softening dry skin overnight.

Put the lanolin, beeswax and almond oil into a heatproof bowl and stand it over a saucepan of simmering water. Gently stir the ingredients until they melt.

In another bowl, put the borax. Heat the bottled water in a separate pan and pour it over the borax. Stir well and add the lanolin mixture to it.

Pierce the wheatgerm capsules and stir these into the creamy mixture. Finally, add the essential oil and stir thoroughly with a metal spoon so that it is well distributed.

The cream should be put straight into a container with a tight-fitting lid before it begins to set. Store it in a cool place or the door of a refrigerator.

PEACH AND MARIGOLD FACE PACK

1 fresh peach
10 marigold flowerheads
Ground almonds

Marigolds have long been known for their soothing properties on skin irritated by fierce sun or wind. Here is a simple recipe for a fruity mask which will help to freshen and soften the whole face.

Pick the petals from each flowerhead and put them into a food processor. Then peel the peach and slice the flesh into small pieces. Add the peach to the petals and process them quickly. Finally, stir in enough ground almonds to make a thick paste. Apply the pack to clean skin, avoiding your eyes, and leave for 15 minutes before rinsing it off with warm water. Keep any extra face pack in the refrigerator.

The healing properties of marigold petals have long been exploited. Here they combine with fresh peach and almonds to make a soothing, skin softening face mask.

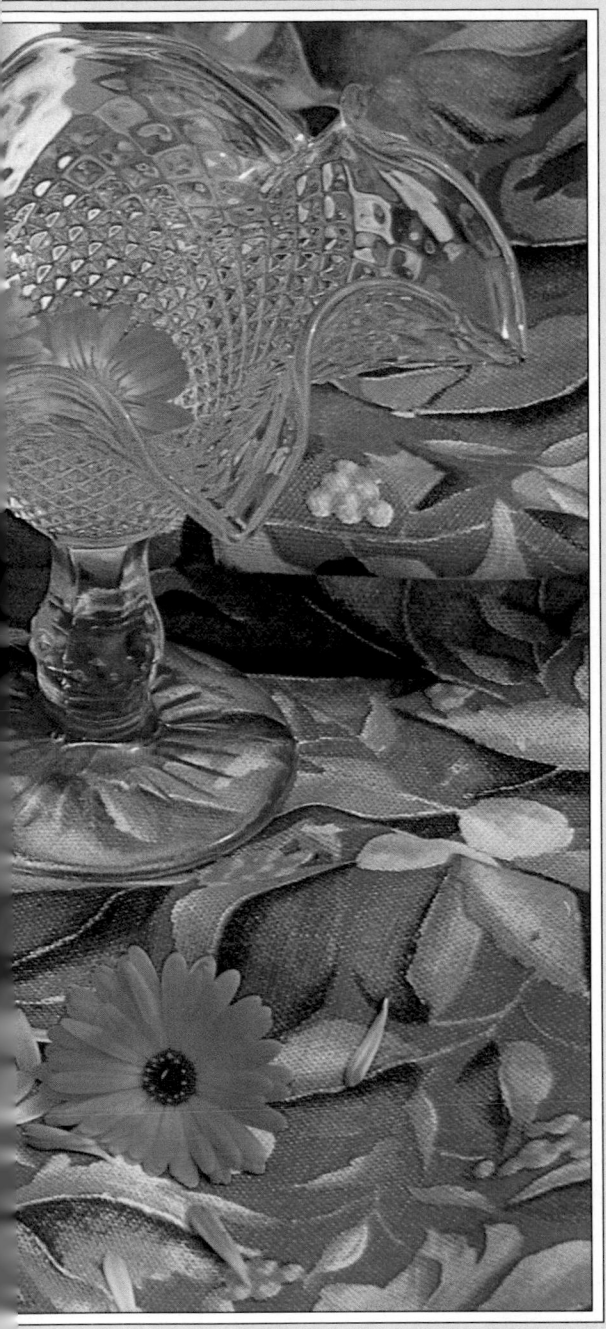

Pour the oats into a mixing bowl. If you prefer to make a finer mask, you can process the oats in a food processor or blender for a few seconds first.

Add the rosewater to the oats, working the mixture into a paste. Watch the consistency — if the mask is too thin or too thick, it will simply slide off your face.

Finally, add 2 drops of rose essential oil and mix the paste thoroughly.

To use, apply the mask to the face, avoiding the areas close to your eyes, and leave for about 15 minutes. Rinse off with lukewarm water and pat your face dry. Finish with a mild toner to close up the pores.

ABOVE: Dried marigold petals combine with natural yoghurt to make a therapeutic and uplifting face mask.

MARIGOLD MASK

6 tbsp of dried marigold (any variety) petals
4 tbsp of good quality natural yoghurt
3 tbsp of bottled mineral water
4 tbsp of oatmeal
1 tbsp of wheatgerm

This mask is wonderfully restorative, but it must be applied while it is still warm, so it cannot really be stored.

Put the marigold petals into a bowl, heat the bottled water and pour it over the petals. Add the oatmeal and wheatgerm and stir vigorously. Pour in the yoghurt and continue to mix well.

Making sure the mask is warm but not too hot, apply it to your face, avoiding the eyes. It should be left on for 20-30 minutes and rinsed off with lukewarm water.

ROSEWATER AND OAT FACE MASK

3-4 tbsp of porridge oats
1-2 tbsp of rosewater
2 drops of rose essential oil

This natural face mask is a wonderful cleanser. It helps unclog pores and remove dead cells which make the skin look dull.

LEFT: This mildly abrasive Rosewater and Oat Face Mask sloughs off dead cells to revitalize your skin.

LEFT: *Put into an old-fashioned powder bowl, this lavender and herbal talc gives a luxurious finish to bath – or showertime.*

Bergamot Cologne is a delicious after-bath, splash-on cologne, with a fragrance that is suitable for men or women.

Take the rose and carnation, strip off all the petals and put them into a screw-top jar. Pour the vodka over the petals. Screw the top on to the jar, shake well and leave the mixture to stand on a sunny windowsill for about a week.

When the petals are ready, bring the bottled water to the boil. Put the orange peel and cloves into a bowl and pour the boiling water over them. Leave this mixture to stand for about 5-6 hours.

Strain both the petal/vodka mixture and the orange/clove mixture through a fine sieve into a glass jug. Check for clarity. You may find that the mixture needs straining again through a finer sieve or a coffee filter paper to clear it completely.

Finally, add the bergamot essential oil drop by drop and stir well. Decant the mixture into a sterilized bottle and keep in a cool place between use.

HERBAL TALCUM POWDER

5 tbsp of lavender flowers or any other
perfumed flowers of your choice
2 tbsp of dried, chopped mixed herbs
10 tbsp unscented talcum powder
1 tbsp of lavender essential oil

As a welcome change to ready-scented talcum powder, why not buy the unperfumed type and add your own scents?

This recipe uses lavender and herbs, but you could experiment using other kinds of fresh flowers such as roses or jasmine combined with their matching essential oils.

Put the lavender flowers (or the flowers of your choice) and the mixed herbs into a blender or food processor and process them to a fine powder. You will find that this is quite a lengthy process, but it needs to be done thoroughly.

First, sieve the talcum powder into a bowl and add the powdered lavender and herbs. Then add the essential oil carefully, mixing it in thoroughly before transferring the powder to an old-fashioned powder bowl or other shallow container with a lid.

BERGAMOT COLOGNE

1 fresh, sweet-scented rose
1 scented carnation
4fl oz (115ml) of cheap vodka
3 tbsp of dried orange peel (zest)
1 tsp of cloves
½ pt (350ml) of bottled mineral water
3 drops of bergamot essential oil

Infused with cloves, orange and petals, this Bergamot Cologne has a fresh fragrance, ideal for après bathtime.

ABOVE: Leafy Aftershave makes the ideal gift with its subtle fragrance and mildly astringent properties.

LEAFY AFTERSHAVE

3 tbsp of dried strawberry leaves
3½ fl oz (100ml) of bottled mineral water
4fl oz (115ml) of rosewater
1 tsp of borax

A fine gift for the men in your life, this subtle, leafy splash-on is best kept stored in the refrigerator.

Put the strawberry leaves into a heatproof bowl. In a small saucepan, bring the bottled mineral water to the boil and pour over the strawberry leaves. Let this solution infuse for about 4-5 hours.

Then pour the rosewater into another heatproof bowl. Set this over a saucepan of simmering water and heat the rosewater through. When it's hot, add the borax, stirring very gently until all the borax has dissolved. Remove from the heat.

To the rosewater and borax mixture add the strawberry leaf solution, straining it first through a fine sieve in order to remove all traces of the leaves.

Finally, pour the aftershave into an attractive, sterilized bottle.

LAVENDER AND MINT FOOT BATH

3½ pt (2 litres) of bottled mineral water
3 stems of fresh peppermint or 1 tbsp of dried
6 stems of fresh lavender or 2 tbsp of dried
1 or 2 drops of lavender essential oil

Using fragrant lavender and mint flowers, this foot bath is a quick, effective pick-me-up for tired, aching feet. If you prefer, you could try using rosemary as a refreshing alternative to lavender.

First, heat 10fl oz (300ml) of mineral water to boiling point and pour this over the flowers in a small bowl or jug. Leave the mixture to infuse for at least 15 minutes, then strain into a large bowl.

Add the oil, stir well and top up with the rest of the warm water .

BELOW: A lavender and peppermint foot bath, here infusing before use, is a wonderful refresher for aching feet.

$\mathcal{F}$LORAL GIFTS

*A range of pretty stationery can be easily
scented to make a most welcome gift.*

In this chapter you will find ways of using dried
flowers, pressed flowers and pot-pourri to make a
selection of lovely gifts. From simple scented
sachets and notepaper to more complex wardrobe
sets, there's something for everyone to
enjoy making and giving.

This notepaper and envelope set has been stored with lavender bundles to give it a distinctive fragrance.

Most of the gift ideas on the following pages use materials that are readily available, such as scraps of fabric and ribbon, little boxes or stationery. By adding a few dried flowers, some home-made pot-pourri or a pretty pressed-flower design, you have an individual and highly personalized gift which will delight anyone.

LAVENDER SCENTED PAPER

Dried lavender flowerheads
1 tsp of orris root powder
2 or 3 drops of lavender essential oil
Lavender coloured notepaper and envelopes
Net
Ribbon or fine wire

Perfume readily available stationery with a matching fragrance for a delightful gift. The notepaper and envelopes are simply stored together with a strong pot-pourri which imparts its fragrance to the paper.

First make the pot-pourri. Mix the dried lavender together with the orris root and the essential oil, stirring well with a metal spoon until all the oil has been well dispersed among the flowers.

Make little sachets by cutting out several circles of net. Fill each one with the pot-pourri and secure tightly with a ribbon or piece of wire. Place these net bundles into a box containing the stationery and leave for at least one week, longer if possible, before repackaging the gift.

Stick a few stems of lavender on to the lid of the box for a finishing touch.

TEDDY PINCUSHION

Pot-pourri (see recipes on pages 88-97)
10in (25cm) circle of lace fabric
8in (20cm) circle of cotton fabric
Scraps of lace and ribbon
Polyester wadding
Needle and thread
Small toy teddy or doll

This little teddy makes a charming gift and can be used simply for decoration if not as a pincushion.

Line the lace fabric with the cotton, neatly stitching the two together. Then sew running stitch around the edge of the lace circle, leaving the end of the thread loose for gathering later. Lay the circle lace side down, and put some wadding on top. Thenplace the teddy in the centre of the wadding and add the pot-pourri.

Pull the running stitch tight to gather up the lace circle around the teddy's waist, and fasten off firmly. Make two shoulder

BELOW: This little teddy's skirt emits a lovely fragrance and makes a practical pincushion as well as a cute decoration.

straps from ribbon or lace, securing them with a couple of stitches. Finally, decorate the cushion with lace gathered around the teddy's waist, finishing off with a bow.

SWEET BAG

For the sweet bag mixture:
1 cup of strongly scented dried rose petals
1 cup of dried lavender
$\frac{1}{2}$ cup of dried lemon verbena leaves
$\frac{1}{2}$ cup of crushed dried rosemary
2 tbsp of orris root powder
2 crushed cinnamon sticks
3 drops of rose essential oil

For the bag:
Fine, lace edged, cotton lawn handkerchief
Bright check ribbon

ABOVE: For quick results, make a pretty sweet bag from a lacy handkerchief.

A sweet bag is an old-fashioned term for a scented drawer or linen sachet. The one shown here is the simplest of all to make, requiring no sewing. Use the recipe here for the filling, or choose any of the other pot-pourri recipes on pages 88-97.

Make the filling by mixing together all the dry ingredients in a large bowl using a metal spoon. Add the essential oil, and stir well. Put the mixture in a sealed container, give it a shake, then leave it in a dark place for about four weeks.

When the mixture is ready, pour it into the centre of the lace handkerchief. Gather the handkerchief up around the pot-pourri and tie it firmly with ribbon.

ADDRESS BOOK

Pressed white larkspur buds and leaves
Plain black address book
Tweezers
Latex adhesive
Self-adhesive protective film

Enhance a plain black address book with a column of pressed white flowers to make an attractive gift.

First, place the largest larkspur bud at the bottom edge of the book, about ½ in (1cm) in from both edges. Fix with a dab of adhesive. With the aid of the tweezers, gently position the flowers up the book, using buds of decreasing size, and angling them to give interest. Secure each one with a little adhesive.

When the design is complete, seal it with a strip of protective film. The film should measure the height of the book, plus a 1in (2.5cm) overlap, and the width of the design, plus ½ in (1cm). Finally, rub the film down carefully, turning in the overlap on all three sides.

BELOW: Dress up a black address book by decorating it with pressed larkspur flowers.

FRAGRANT HOT WATER BOTTLE

Quilted floral fabric and lining fabric
Other scraps of fabric
Contrasting sewing thread
Satin ribbon
Herbal pot-pourri (for recipes see pages 88-97)

Herbs and flowers are often used to relax and soothe. The heat from the bottle will help release the soothing fragrance.

Draw around the hot water bottle to make a template and use this to cut out two pieces of quilted fabric and two of lining, allowing extra for a seam allowance.

From the fabric scraps, cut out three or four flower shapes. Using machine zig-zag stitch, appliqué these to one of the quilted bottle shapes. From another fabric scrap, cut a basket shape and handle. Sew these in

This scented hot water bottle cover has a sachet tucked into its appliquéd pocket.

front of the flowers as shown, leaving the top of the basket open to form a pocket.

Stitch the lining to the right side of the quilted fabric, leaving a gap, and turn out. Repeat to make the back of the cover, then hand-stitch the gaps closed. Then with right sides together, stitch both the bottle shapes together, leaving an opening at the 'shoulders' of the bottle.

For the sachet, cut out two more flower shapes and, wrong sides together, machine zig-zag around the edges, leaving a small gap to fill the sachet with pot-pourri. Stitch up the opening. Tuck this flower sachet into the 'basket' and, to finish, add a little bow to the opening at the top of the bottle.

PERFUME POCKET

Pot-pourri (for recipes, see pages 88-97)
Small cushion and cover made
with floral fabric
Scrap of fabric to match or complement
the cushion cover
Narrow satin ribbon
Needle and thread
Pins

A pretty floral cushion, complete with a pocket and scented sachet, makes a superb gift. You can either make your own cushion cover, or buy one and team up a scrap of fabric to make the pocket and sachet.

Cut a rectangle from the scrap of fabric to sit on the front of the cushion. As a general guide, if your cushion measures 12in (30cm) square, the pocket should measure about 3in by 4in (7.5cm by 10cm). Turn under one long edge and hem. Turn under the other three sides and press. Pin the rectangle to the front of the cushion cover, while keeping the hemmed edge at the top. Neatly stitch the pocket to the cover.

To make the sachet, cut a long rectangle of fabric. (To fit the pocket measurements

A scented sachet is kept in a pocket sewn to one side of this pretty cushion.

above, the rectangle will need to be 10in by 3in (25cm by 7.5cm).) With wrong sides together, fold the rectangle in half and stitch up both long sides. Turn right sides out and hem around the top edge.

Fill the sachet with your chosen pot-pourri and tie the sachet with the ribbon. Tuck it into the cushion pocket to complete.

You can easily renew the pot-pourri if it loses its fragrance.

the opening. Add a satin ribbon bow to the top as a finishing touch.

The hanger and shoe shapes also have little fabric flowers stitched on to them. To make one flower, cut two flower shapes from the contrast fabric, place them wrong sides together and machine zig-zag around the edges. Add a little decorative stitch to the centre to finish.

INSECT DETERRENT

3 cups of dried santolina or
cotton lavender
1 tbsp of cloves
1 tbsp of caraway seeds
1 tbsp of mace
3 cinnamon sticks
Calico
String or twine

This makes a really useful present, especially during a hot summer! And it's so easy to create. Simply crush the cinnamon sticks in a bowl and mix with the other dry ingredients. Cut out several 10in (25cm) circles of calico and fill each one with a tablespoon of the spicy mixture. To complete, gather up the sides and tie with string.

FRAGRANT WARDROBE SET

For the pot-pourri:
1 cup of dried lavender
1 cup of dried crumbled southernwood
½ cup of dried crumbled rosemary
2 crushed cinnamon sticks
Other materials:
Plain coat hanger
Floral fabric
Contrasting thread
Narrow ribbon to match the thread
Fabric scrap the same colour as the thread
Wadding and polyester stuffing

If you are handy with a needle and thread, you will enjoy making this pretty matching wardrobe set which consists of a scented hanger, sachet and shoe shapes.

First make the pot-pourri by combining all the ingredients. It is not necessary to leave this mixture to cure.

To make the hanger, mix the pot-pourri with some stuffing and wrap this around the hanger. Secure the scented stuffing to

ABOVE: A Fragrant Wardrobe Set makes a charming gift. It consists of a scented hanger, sachet and shoe shapes.

the hanger by winding thread around and around it. Line a piece of floral fabric with fine wadding and machine quilt. Use this to cover the hanger. Add a little satin bow by the hook.

For the sachet, cut out two butterfly shapes from the floral fabric and, with wrong sides together, machine zig-zag the edges. Leave a little gap and fill with pot-pourri and a little stuffing. Stitch up the gap and add a tiny ribbon bow to the front and a hanging ribbon loop.

The shoe shapes are made from oval-shaped pieces of floral fabric. Make sure that the shapes will comfortably fit inside your shoes.

Stitch two pieces of the fabric, right sides together, leaving a small gap to turn the shape right sides out. Pack the shape with stuffing and pot-pourri before stitching up

BELOW: This is an unusual, but most useful, gift. These little bags contain a practical Insect Deterrent.

BERGAMOT AND ORANGE SACHET

Dried orange peel (zest)
Dried hebe leaves
2 tsp of orris root powder
2-3 drops of bergamot essential oil
10in (25cm) circle of lace fabric
1⅛ yd (l metre) of pre-gathered edging lace
1yd (90cm) of narrow peach
coloured ribbon
Needle and thread

This frothy boudoir sachet emits a lovely fragrance, and is really too pretty to tuck away in a drawer. Hang it in the wardrobe or from the mirror of a dressing table. Begin by making the pot-pourri. In a large bowl, mix together the orange peel, leaves, orris root powder and the bergamot oil. Stir well with a metal spoon. For a longer lasting scent, leave this mixture to mature in a sealed container for about a month, shaking it occasionally.

For the sachet, stitch the edging lace to the circle then thread the narrow ribbon through the lace, about lin (2.5cm) in from the edge. Next, pull the ribbon to gather the edges of the lace into a bag shape. Fill the sachet with pot-pourri, gather the ribbon tightly and secure with a pretty bow.

BELOW: This lacy bundle emits a warm scent of bergamot and orange.

ABOVE: Choose a favourite special fragrance to make this pretty Perfume Pot.

PERFUME POT

Pressed flowers and leaves; used here are variegated geranium leaves, silverweed, yellow medick and wood avens
Small ceramic pot with lid that dismantles
3 tsp of shredded beeswax
2 tsp of almond oil
15 drops of concentrated essential oil of your choice
Drop of sap-green dye
Latex adhesive

This solid perfume is simple to make and looks so pretty in a matching ceramic jar—a perfect complement to any dressing table.

Begin by creating the floral design on the insert card supplied with the lid. Fix the foliage in place first with the adhesive to create a triangular shape (see pages 73-85 for more details). Follow this outline with the other flowers. Here, the bold flowerheads of the wood avens have been used as the focal point of the display.

To make the perfume, melt the wax and almond oil in a saucepan over a very low heat. Remove the pan and, when the mixture has cooled a little, add the perfume oil and dye and pour it into the trinket pot. It will then set hard and be ready for use.

LACE-TRIMMED SACHET

For the pot-pourri:
l cup of dried rose petals
l cup of dried lavender
½ cup of dried crushed rosemary
2 crushed sticks of cinnamon
2 tbsp of orris root powder
3 drops of rose essential oil

These feminine lace-trimmed sachets make perfect dressing table accessories.

For the sachet:
Two 5in (13cm) circles of fine cotton lawn
20in (50cm) of cotton lace
Ribbon rose
Narrow satin ribbon
Matching thread and needle

These exquisite lace-trimmed sachets are designed for scenting dressing table drawers and they make lovely gifts for female friends or relatives.

First make the pot-pourri by mixing all the dry ingredients in a large bowl. Add the essential oil and mix thoroughly. Put the mixture into a sealed container, shake well, and leave for about four weeks. (For other pot-pourri recipes see pages 86-97.)

To make the sachet, place the cotton circles, right sides together, and stitch around the edge, leaving a small gap. Turn the sachet right side out and press. Fill with the pot-pourri, taking care not to over-stuff the sachet and make it too bulky. Sew up the opening. Now add the lace edging, stitching it on neatly by hand. Finally, stitch on the ribbon rose and narrow ribbon.

LAVENDER BOTTLES

Long stems of fresh lavender
Narrow lavender coloured ribbon or string

Lavender bottles are a charming and old-fashioned way of keeping clothes fresh and sweet smelling. Package some in a pretty basket as a delightful gift idea.

The method used to make the bottles is quite simple but you may need a little practice. Gather together a bunch of the lavender and tie a narrow piece of ribbon directly under the lavender heads.

Gently bend each stem back separately to encase the lavender heads and make a small cage. Tie another length of ribbon around the stems. Leave a loop of ribbon hanging so the lavender can dry naturally.

LEFT: These old-fashioned Lavender Bottles are an excellent way of keeping linen and clothes fresh and sweet smelling.

ABOVE: Treat someone to a tried and tested remedy for fine wooden furniture with a pot of this fragrant Lavender Furniture Polish.

LAVENDER FURNITURE POLISH

$\frac{2}{3}$ cup of turpentine
$\frac{2}{3}$ cup of linseed oil
$\frac{1}{3}$ cup of cider vinegar
$\frac{1}{3}$ cup of methylated spirits
10 drops of lavender essential oil
Screw-top jar and gift jar

This beautifully fragrant polish makes an unusual but welcome gift to lovers of fine wooden furniture. The polish feeds wood and buffs to a really good shine.

Pour all the ingredients into the screw-top jar, screw the lid on tightly and shake really thoroughly. When mixed, pour into the gift jar and secure the cork. Finally, add a gift tag listing the ingredients and a note explaining the nature of the contents.

POSY BOXES

*Dried, small-headed flowers such as
larkspur, sunray, small roses, golden rod,
amaranthus, gypsophila (baby's breath)
Fine florists' wire
Satin or gift ribbon
All-purpose glue*

A delicate posy of dried flowers provides
a perfect decoration for any gift. It can also
be detached from the present and kept as
an additional memento. Match the flowers
to the giftwrap by choosing complemen-
tary colours. Alternatively, you could use
plain giftwrap and any floral combination.

Gather a selection of dried flowers together and arrange them into an attractive
shape. Bind the stems together firmly with
wire. Now wrap ribbon around the stems
to cover the wire and finish off with a bow.
Attach the posy to the gift with glue.

GILDED BAY LEAVES

*Nuts and whole dried bay leaves
Gold giftwrap
Wide ribbon and gold cord
Metallic paint in two or three colours
Hot glue gun or all-purpose glue*

*Create a really special present by decorating
your gift with golden bay leaves.*

Dried flowers and leaves give a wrapped
present an extra special finishing touch.

First, paint the bay leaves on both sides
with the metallic paint. Use bronze, copper
and gold paints for a range of different
finishes. Leave the leaves to dry completely
on a wire cooling rack used for baking.

Wrap the gift with gold paper and tie it
with wide giftwrap or satin ribbon, finishing with a generous bow. Tuck the gold
cord into this ribbon bow and then tie the
gold cord in a little bow. For speedy results,
use a hot glue gun to stick the gilded leaves
to the ribbon. Stick on a few nuts as well.

FLOWERY GIFT BOXES

*A selection of small boxes
Magazine and seed catalogue cut-outs
Floral wallpaper or giftwrap
All-purpose glue or double-sided tape
Clear varnish
Dried flowers (optional)*

*ABOVE: Make a selection of Posy Boxes for
extra-special gift wrapped presents.*

*RIGHT: This simple circular box filled with
pot-pourri has been covered with a selection
of colourful flower pictures. Each one over-
laps the other to give a dense and rich effect.*

Small boxes are ideal for gifts and they can
be decorated in a number of ways.

Try covering a box with cut-outs from
magazines and seed catalogues to create a
pretty floral surface. Overlap the pictures
to give a solid mass of colour. This tech-
nique is known as découpage. Always coat
the finished box with clear varnish to seal
the pictures. A simpler method is to cover a
box with a piece of good quality floral wallpaper or giftwrap. Either coat the wrong
side of the paper with adhesive and glue it
to the box, or use double-sided tape.

If you wish, you can finish off with a
spray of dried flowers on the box lid.

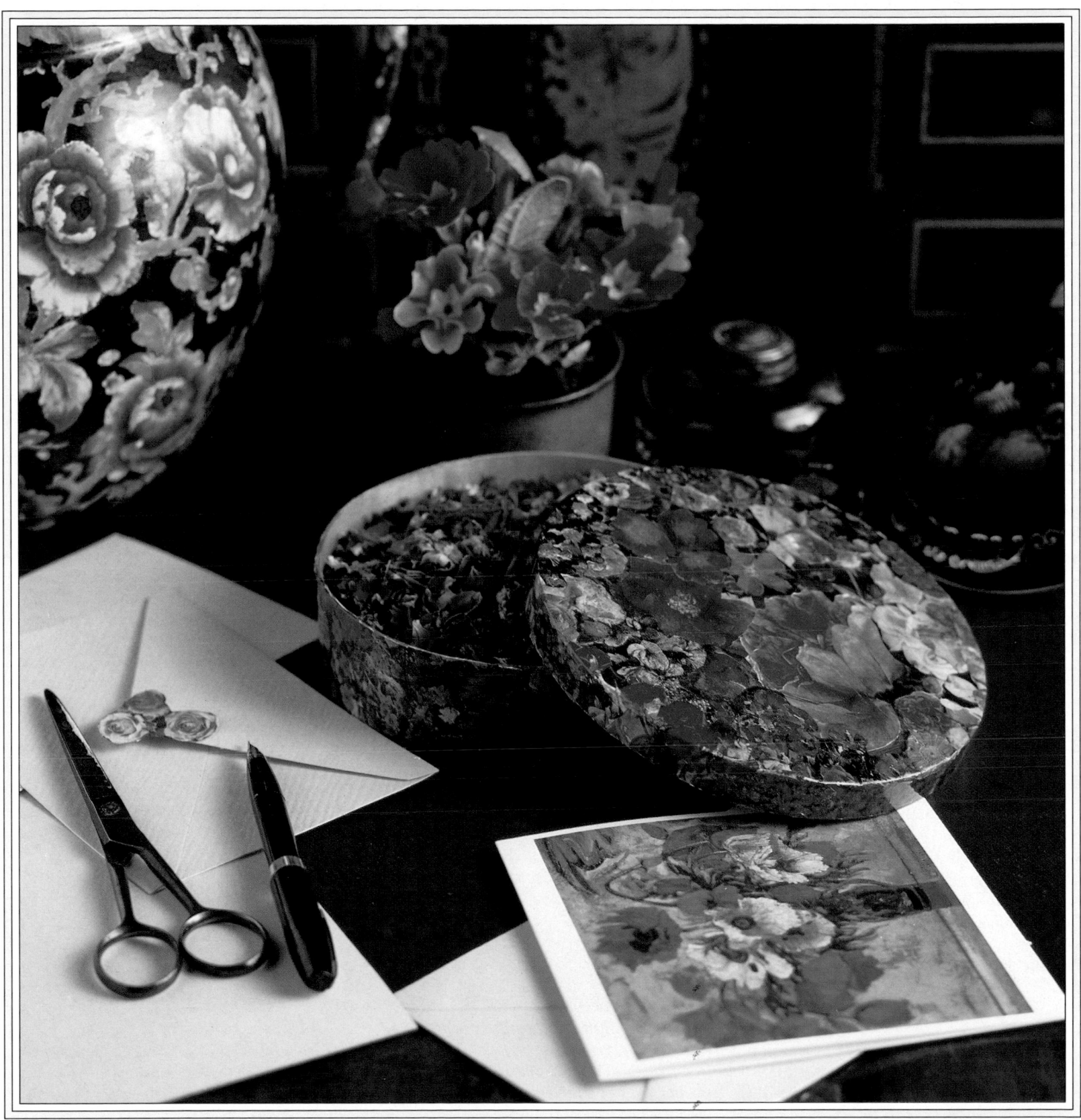

FLOWER CARE

Garden flowers are best cut in the early morning or evening, when transpiration is at its lowest. On a hot, sunny afternoon, they will naturally have less moisture in their cells and therefore be more prone to wilt.

As flowers always benefit from a long drink before they are used, this may determine just when they are gathered. Ideally, a drink overnight is perfect if they are to be used the next morning, so evening picking is probably best.

Always gather flowers quickly and put them into water as soon as possible. Choose fresh, healthy blooms just coming into full flower, or in slightly open bud.

Some flowers naturally last longer than others , but all can be prolonged with care. Condition the flowers as described below.

BUYING FLOWERS

Shop-bought flowers are usually conditioned before they are sold, but you can still re-cut the stems under water yourself. Once trimmed, give the flowers a long drink for a few hours before transferring them to shallow water and a warm room.

In the spring and summer there generally will be more choice of flowers available. The flowers are also likely to be less expensive than in the winter, when most of the florist's stock will either have been imported or grown in hot-house conditions.

Make sure you buy flowers from a shop or stall that has a quick turnover and fresh supplies brought in from markets at least twice a week.

Whenever you buy flowers, remember the golden rule is to look for good, crisp foliage, strong, straight stems and tight, firm flower buds.

CONDITIONING FLOWERS

1 Cut flower stems at a sharp angle, so that the maximum area of the cut end is exposed to the water. Do this under water if possible.

2 Peel back a little of the bark of woody stems of shrubs and trees, then hammer or split the first inch or so to allow the water to penetrate easily. This can be done with a hammer, sharp garden secateurs or strong scissors.

3 Stand the prepared flowers in a bucket filled with warm water and leave them to have a long drink for several hours or overnight. If the stems are bent and you want to straighten them, wrap the flowers tightly in newspaper and plunge into water. This method is effective for flowers such as tulips and gerbera.

4 Certain flowers exude a milky sap which interferes with their water intake. The stems of flowers such as poppies, euphorbia and ferns can be sealed by singeing the ends over a flame.

5 *The large, hollow stems of flowers such as delphiniums and amaryllis (Hippeastrum) can be filled with water and then plugged with a small piece of cotton wool. Stand the stems in water straight after this treatment.*

7 *Roses should have all their thorns removed, as well as any extra leaves and small branches. Strip the thorns off the stems with the blade of a pair of scissors, or use a tool available specially for this purpose.*

9 *If flowers wilt unexpectedly, try reviving them by recutting the stems and standing them in shallow hot water for about half an hour. Position the flowers away from the steam when adding the water.*

6 *Always strip the lower leaves off stems so that they do not sit under water in the vase. Rotting leaves will pollute the water and encourage the creation of bacteria, cloudy water and an unpleasant smell.*

8 *Some lilies have pollen-laden stamens that can brush against clothes and furnishings and stain indelibly. To prevent this from happening, carefully snip out the stamens using a little pair of manicure scissors.*

10 *Remove the topmost buds of flowers such as gladioli to ensure that the lower buds open. Condition foliage by immersing it in water for a few hours. Do not do this on grey- or silver-leaved foliage, or on plants with woolly foliage.*

TOOLS AND EQUIPMENT

CUTTING TOOLS

Essential tools for flower arranging are a pair of good-quality secateurs or florists' scissors with short blades. Also useful are scissors with a special wire-cutting notch.

WATERING EQUIPMENT

A long-spouted watering can is useful for reaching into large arrangements to top them up with clean water. Many flowers enjoy a fine hazy mist of water, so include a spray mister among your equipment.

TAPE

For posies and bouquets you may need the special tape for binding stems and wrapping around wires. Often known as gutta-percha tape, it comes in green, white and brown. Florists' adhesive tape is also available for sticking foam shapes together.

FLORISTS' FOAM

Blocks of wet foam for supporting fresh flowers in shallow containers are indispensable, as are blocks of the special type of foam available for dried flower arrangements. Both types of foam can be cut to any shape and size, and can easily be concealed, if necessary, with a layer of moss.

Most of the wet foam available today can be soaked in a minute or so. Allow the foam to stand above the edge of your container if you wish to add extra height to the flowers. Tape or wire the foam in position if necessary, or push it down on to a special florists' spike anchored with adhesive clay to the bottom of the container.

Foam does not look good in glass containers unless it is covered or hidden in some way, so save these for simple and informal arrangements.

WIRE

Different kinds of wire are useful. Stiff stub wire is excellent for dried flower displays, and a reel of fine rose wire is handy for many jobs. Wire mesh can be used as a support for large and heavy stems in a vase.

If cut at an angle, most stems will push easily into damp foam and will stay firmly put. However, if you are using plants with very soft stems you may need to spike holes first in the foam, into which the stems can then be inserted.

Flowers take up a lot of water, so remember to keep the foam damp by topping up the container with fresh water occasionally, particularly in warm conditions.

SUPPORTS FOR PLANTS

FUNNELS

If you are planning a really grand, large-scale arrangement for a special occasion, long funnels will be useful for adding extra height to individual flower stems.

PINHOLDERS

Pinholders are heavy, metal blocks with sharp spikes and are a good way of securing some arrangements. Attach them to the base of the container with florists' putty, then insert the flowers among the spikes.

WIRE MESH

Crumpled wire mesh is very useful for supporting plants in wide-necked vases and shallow bowls, particularly if you are using large, woody-stemmed branches and top-heavy flowers. It can be jammed in place, or wired or taped inside the container.

MARBLES

Clear glass marbles make a pretty addition to a glass vase and they help hold stems in position. Clean, scrubbed pebbles can also be used for the same purpose.

TWIGS

To secure stems in exactly the right position in a container, cut a twig into small pieces and use these as a wedge or prop.

PROLONGING THE LIFE OF AN ARRANGEMENT

If your flowers have been conditioned well and are arranged in damp foam or water, they should last for a week or more depending on the variety. To help them last longer, always remember to keep the parts of the stems that are under water free from leaves, and use slightly warm water, never icy cold. Add a drop or two of bleach and a teaspoon of sugar to the water, or use the special crystals often provided by florists with cut flowers which help to prolong flower life. Replace the water after a few days if it is getting stale and remove and discard any plant material that is obviously tired, fading or dead. Cut out spent blooms and leave the buds to open out.

 151

$\mathcal{F}$LOWERS TO GROW

Growing your own flowers is a very satisfying and absorbing hobby. It also makes gathering flowers and foliage for the projects in this book a lot less expensive. A garden is not vital to grow many varieties. Patios with pots and troughs, window boxes or small courtyards can all yield a wealth of material.

The following chart is a guide to growing your own plants. It has been divided into four major categories: fresh, dried, pressed and edible flowers. Many flowers can successfully be used in all these categories – roses, for example, are extremely versatile. Generally, each section gives a list of suitable plants, a brief description, and the best environment for growing them. It also gives the natural flowering seasons. The plants are listed alphabetically by Latin name. If you have trouble finding a plant and know it by its common name, look at the Scientific Classification chart on page 166.

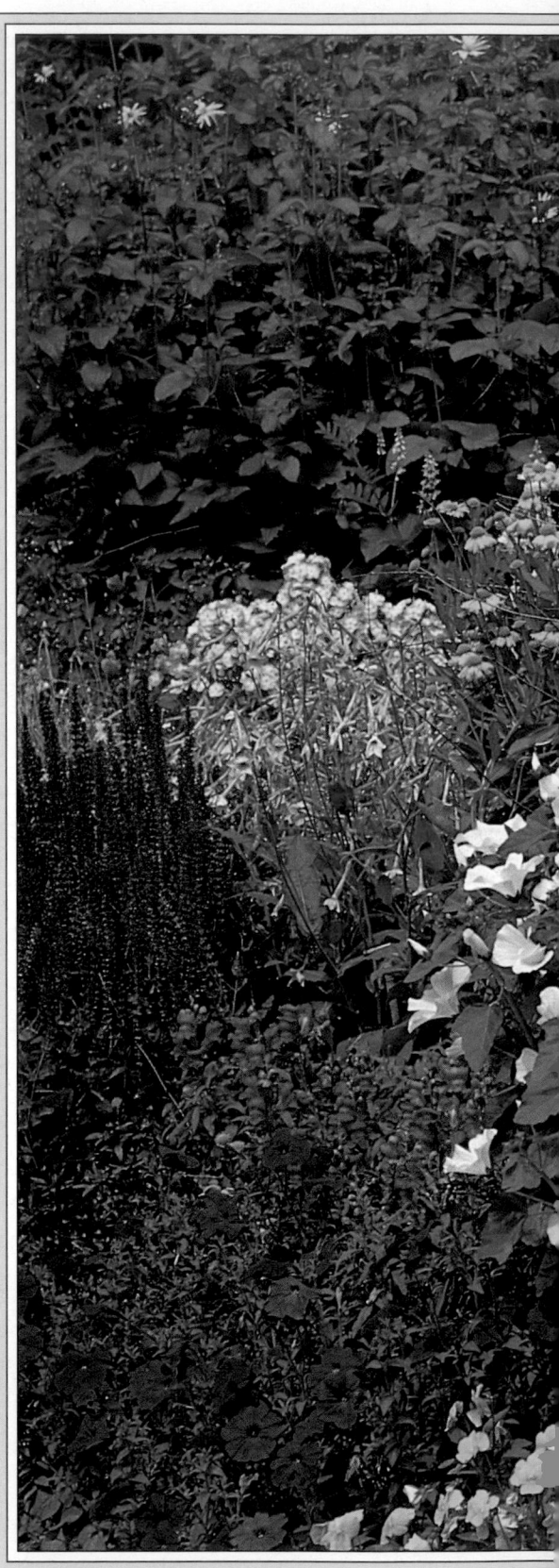

RIGHT: *A well-planned border is not only decorative, it can provide a wealth of material for the projects and recipes featured in this book.*

FRESH FLOWERS

Name	Type/description	Cultivation/ Flowering season	Conditioning when cut
Iris sp. Flag	Ruffled flowers on tall stems with lower petals ('falls'). Many colours, usually blue-purple and yellow. Very hardy evergreen rhizome.	Moist, neutral/ lime-free soil in full sun. Blooms spring and early summer.	Cut stems on slant, give long drink.
	Also herbaceous *Iris* grown from bulb. More slender and delicate.	Light, well-drained soil in full sun and shelter. Plant early autumn. Blooms late winter/spring.	As above.
Lilium sp. Lily	Most colours except blue. Trumpet-shaped, stately flowers. Very hardy bulb.	Well-drained soil in sun/partial shade. Plant autumn/early spring. Flowers early summer.	Cut stems on slant and give drink in cold water.
Moluccella laevis Bells of Ireland	Distinctive, tall, all-green plant. Half-hardy annual.	Light, rich, well-drained soil in full sun. Flowers summer.	Strip off most foliage. Put stems in $\frac{1}{2}$ in of boiling water for 2 mins. Then give long cool drink.
Myosotis sylvatica Forget-me-not	Usually blue with white eye, also pink. Moderately hardy and grown as a biennial.	Fertile soil, generally sun. Blooms spring and early summer.	Cut stems, give long drink.
Narcissus sp. Daffodil/narcissus	Yellow, orange or white trumpet-shaped flower with outer petals. Very hardy perennial.	Well-drained soil in sun or partial shade. Plant bulbs late summer/early autumn. Blooms in spring.	Cut stems, put in cool, shallow water. Keep apart from other flowers for 24 hours as stems produce poison which kills other plants.

FRESH FLOWERS			
NAME	TYPE/DESCRIPTION	CULTIVATION/ FLOWERING SEASON	CONDITIONING WHEN CUT
Paeonia sp. Peony	Red, white or pink, multi-petalled. Very hardy perennial.	Rich, well-drained soil in sun. Blooms early – mid-summer.	Cut ends, give long drink of warm water.
Ranunculus asiaticus Persian buttercup	Plump, cup-shaped, multi-petalled flowers in yellow orange, pink, red and white. Moderately hardy tuber.	Very good drainage, full sun. Plant early spring. Flowers late spring/ summer.	Cut ends, dip in boiling water, then give long drink.
Rosa sp. Rose	Wide variety of roses for easy growing in virtually every colour and shape. Grown as bushes, standards or climbers.	Well-drained soil with sun for several hours a day. Blooms generally in summer.	Crush ends with hammer, place in boiling water then give long drink. Can be revived with teaspoon of sugar.
Scabiosa sp. Scabious/ Pincushion flower	Daisy-like flowers with overlapping petals. Usually mauve-blue, also pink and white. Ultra-hardy perennial.	Likes sun. May need support. Flowers in summer.	Cut stems and give overnight drink.
Tulipa sp. Tulip	Bold colours, cup/goblet-shaped, six-petalled, single flowers. Also double varieties. Very hardy bulb.	Rich, well-drained soil in sun. Plant bulb mid autumn/early winter. Lift bulb when foliage dies, store till autumn. Blooms in spring.	Cut stems, wrap flowers in stiff paper for two hours. Place in shallow water.

DRIED FLOWERS			
NAME	TYPE/DESCRIPTION	CULTIVATION/ FLOWERING SEASON	METHOD OF PRESERVATION
Achillea sp. Yarrow	Flattish clusters of yellow flowers. Very hardy perennial.	Well-drained soil in full sun. Flowers early – late summer.	Air
Allium sp. Ornamental onion/ ornamental garlic	Small flowers in spheres. Usually blue or pink. Very hardy.	Easy in any well-drained, even poor, soil in sun or partial shade. Flowers early – mid-summer.	Air. Hang upside down until nearly dry. Then stand in tall container so that flowerhead regains shape.
Amaranthus caudatus Loves-lies-bleeding	Erect or drooping tassel-like flowers. Crimson or green. Half-hardy annual.	Any ordinary soil in sun. Flowers in summer.	Air
Anaphalis sp. Pearl everlasting	Silver- or grey-leaved plant with yellow-eyed white flowers in bunched heads. Hardy perennial.	Light, well-drained soil in sun. Flowers mid – late summer.	Air
Carthamus tinctorius Safflower	Thistle-like flowers in deep orange-yellow. Hardy annual.	Ordinary well-drained soil in full sun. Flowers mid-summer.	Air
Cynara scolymus Globe artichoke	Fat, thistle-like vegetable which dries beautifully Moderately hardy.	Well-drained soil in sun. Flowers mid-summer.	Air. Push short stems through wire mesh to support heads while drying.
Delphinium sp. Delphinium	see Fresh Flowers	see Fresh Flowers	Desiccant
Dipsacus sativus (Dipsacus fullonum) Teasel	Lavender coloured flowers which turn into heads of hooked prickles. Hardy biennial.	Rich, moist soil in sun or partial shade. Blooms early summer.	Air, or if still green, glycerine.

DRIED FLOWERS			
NAME	TYPE/DESCRIPTION	CULTIVATION/ FLOWERING SEASON	METHOD OF PRESERVATION
Helichrysum bracteactum Strawflower/ everlasting/ immortelle	Daisy-like, papery flowers in red, orange, pink and yellow. Grown as half-hardy annual.	Light or poor soil in full sun. Flowers in summer.	Air. Wire stem and head before drying.
Helipterum sp. Sunray/immortelle	Daisy-like, fragile flower. Red, rose pink and white. Hardy annual.	Light or poor soil in full sun. Flowers in summer.	Air
Hydrangea sp. Hydrangea	Shrub with lacy flowerheads usually pink or purple-blue. Moderately hardy.	Rich, moist soil in semi or light shade. Best sheltered. Flowers summer into autumn.	Air dry, while allowing stem to be in a little water. Do not replenish, but allow to dry to a crisp feel.
Lagurus ovatus Hare's tail grass	Egg-shaped, silky grassheads are greenish to creamy white. Hardy annual.	Cultivated garden soil, preferably in sun. Blooms from mid-summer to first frost.	Air
Lavendula sp. Lavender	Fragrant grey-blue flowers in spikes on slender stems. Moderately hardy dwarf shrub.	Light, well-drained even poor soil in warm, sunny spot. Flowers late spring/summer.	Air
Limonium sp. Sea lavender	Profuse tiny flowers and ever-green leathery leaves. Blue, white or pink. Ultra-hardy perennial.	Well-drained, fertile soil. Good by the sea. Flowers mid – late summer.	Air
Limonium sinuatum (*Statice sinuata*) Statice	Sprays of yellow, pink, lavender, dark blue and white flowers.	Well-drained, soil in full sun. Usually grown as a half-hardy annual.	Air

DRIED FLOWERS			
NAME	TYPE/DESCRIPTION	CULTIVATION/ FLOWERING SEASON	METHOD OF PRESERVATION
Lunaria annua Honesty/silver dollar	Mauve flowers; flat, circular seedpods. Under the papery cover is a silvery disc. Hardy biennial.	Ordinary, well-drained soil. Will tolerate some shade. Flowers early summer.	Air dry seedpods. Then remove outer casing to reveal striking, pearly-looking discs.
Nigella damascena Love-in-a-mist	Saucer-shaped flowers in blue or pink. Thread-like bracts. Stripy green seedpods. Hardy annual.	Any good soil in sun or partial shade. Sow autumn or early spring. Flowers summer.	Dry seedheads by air.
Paeonia sp. Peony	see Fresh Flowers	See Fresh Flowers	Air/Desiccant
Papaver sp. Poppy	Bold, crepe-like, cup-shaped flowers. Usually red. Moderately hardy. Annual and herbaceous perennial types.	Dry, poor soil in hot sun. Flowers summer.	Dry seedheads by air.
Physalis alkekengi Chinese lantern/ bladder cherry	Bright orange, lantern-like calyces. Ultra-hardy perennial.	Well-drained, fertile soil in full sun. Flowers late summer.	Air
Rosa sp. Rose	see Fresh Flowers	see Fresh Flowers	Air/Dessicant
Solidago sp. Golden rod	Tiny yellow flowers in dense sprays. Ultra-hardy perennial.	Moist, well-drained, fertile soil in sun. Flowers late summer/autumn.	Air

PRESSED FLOWERS			
NAME	TYPE/DESCRIPTION	CULTIVATION/ FLOWERING SEASON	NATURAL SEASON
Alyssum saxatile Gold dust	Trailing rock garden plant with golden yellow flowers.	Well-drained soil in full sun.	Spring to mid-summer.
Centaurea cyanus Cornflower	see Fresh Flowers	see Fresh Flowers	Summer
Delphinium sp. Delphinium	see Fresh Flowers	see Fresh Flowers	Summer
Dianthus sp. Carnations/pinks	see Fresh Flowers	see Fresh Flowers	Summer
Filipendula sp. Meadowsweet	Tall, clump-forming plants with flat-top plumes of tiny flowers. Pink shades. Ultra-hardy herbaceous perennial.	Moist soil in sun or partial shade.	Summer
Iberis umbellata Candytuft	Clusters of white, red or purple flowers. Hardy annual.	Well-drained, moist soil in a sunny position.	Summer

PRESSED FLOWERS			
Name	Type/description	Cultivation/ Flowering season	Natural Season
Lobularia maritima (*Alyssum maritimum*) Sweet Alyssum	Trailing rock plants with profuse white or pink flowers. Very hardy evergreen.	Well-drained, chalky soil in full sun.	Spring and summer.
Montbretia sp. (sometimes listed *Crocosmia sp.*) Montbretia	Bright orange arching spikes of trumpet-shaped flowers and sword-shaped leaves. Hardy corm.	Well-drained soil in full sun. Plant in spring.	From mid-summer.
Myosotis sylvatica Forget-me-not	see Fresh Flowers	see Fresh Flowers	Spring and early summer.
Narcissus sp. Daffodil/narcissus	see Fresh Flowers	see Fresh Flowers	Spring
Polyanthus (sometimes listed *Primula x polyantha*) Polyantha/primula	Primrose-type flowers. Wide colour range. Very to moderately hardy perennial.	Moisture-retentive, fertile soil.	Spring

PRESSED FLOWERS			
NAME	TYPE/DESCRIPTION	CULTIVATION/ FLOWERING SEASON	NATURAL SEASON
Potentilla sp. Cinquefoil	Saucer-shaped flowers and strawberry-type leaves. Usually shades of red and yellow. Very hardy perennial. There are also herbaceous perennial types.	Any soil in full sun.	Summer
Ranunculus sp. Buttercup	Bright yellow, waxy flowers. Very hardy perennial.	Moist soil in sun or light shade.	Late spring/ early summer.
Rosa sp. Rose	see Fresh Flowers	see Fresh Flowers	Summer
Sanguisorba minor *(Poterium sanguisorba)* Salad burnet (Garden burnet)	Reddish-brown stems grow up through leaves, and greenish-red, globular flowers appear at top. Widely grown as a medicinal herb.	Prefers lime soil. In sun or partial shade.	Spring – autumn
Viola sp. Pansy	Asymmetrical round flowers in wide colour range, often bicolour with dark centre. Short-lived perennial treated as hardy annual or half-hardy biennial.	Moist, fertile soil in sun or semi-shade. Good patio, bedding and edging plant.	Summer
Viola tricolor Heart's ease	Tiny pansy, usually cream, yellow or purple-red. Hardy perennial.	Moist soil. Sun or partial shade.	Summer

EDIBLE FLOWERS			
NAME	TYPE/DESCRIPTION	CULTIVATION/ FLOWERING SEASON	NATURAL SEASON
Anthemis nobilis Chamomile	White daisy flowers with yellow eyes.	Light, sandy soil in sunny position.	Summer
Borago officinalis Borage	Coarse, hairy leaves with clusters of deep blue star-shaped flowers. Hardy annual.	Well-drained soil in sun. Sow in early spring.	Summer
Calendula officinalis Marigold	Bright orange/ yellow daisy-like flowers. Hardy annual. Use the single-flowered, pot marigold for cooking.	Most garden soils in a sunny position. Sow early spring.	From early summer through to end of year if climate mild.
Dianthus sp. Carnations/pinks	see Fresh Flowers	see Fresh Flowers	Summer
Lavendula sp. Lavender	see Dried Flowers	see Dried Flowers	Late spring/summer.
Mentha sp. Mint	Fragrant spear-shape leaves in a variety of scents and tastes. Rampant growth.	Moist and dank conditions in sun or shade.	n/a

EDIBLE FLOWERS			
NAME	TYPE/DESCRIPTION	CULTIVATION/ FLOWERING SEASON	NATURAL SEASON
Pelargonium sp. Scented geranium	Highly fragrant leaves with small, usually pink/white flowers. Tender evergreen plants.	Well-drained soil. Likes to be grown from cuttings in pots.	Summer
Primula sp. Primrose	Rosette plants with five-petalled flowers. Yellow, pink and purple. Very hardy.	Moisture-retentive soil and some shade.	Spring and early summer.
Rosa sp. Rose	see Fresh Flowers. Both petals and rose hips can be used in recipes.	see Fresh Flowers	Summer
Thymus sp. Thyme	Aromatic dark green leaves with clusters of mauve flowers.	Well-drained, fertile soil in sun. Replace after 3-4 years.	Summer
Tropaeolum majus Nasturtium	Bright orange/ yellow flowers. Hardy perennial.	Ordinary or poor soil in a sunny position. Sow in spring.	Summer
Viola odorata Sweet violet	Tiny purple flowers. Hardy perennial.	Rich, moisture-retentive but well-drained soil, shielded from fierce sun.	Spring

SCIENTIFIC CLASSIFICATION

The following is an alphabetical list of common names of plants used in this book and their Latin equivalents.

Common name	Latin name
Agrimony	Agrimonia
Alstroemeria	Alstroemeria sp.
Alyssum, sweet	Lobularia maritima (Alyssum maritimum)
Amaryllis	Hippeastrum sp.
Anemone	Anemone sp.
Astrantia	Astrantia sp.
Baby's breath	Gypsophila paniculata
Basil	Ocimum basilicum
Bay, sweet	Laurus nobilis
Beard grass	Polypogon
Bells of Ireland	Molucella laevis
Bergamot	Citrus aurantium bergamia
Bird of paradise	Strelitzia reginae
Borage	Borago officinalis
Bottlebrush	Callistemon sp.
Bouvardia	Bouvardia sp.
Buchu	Agathosma crenulata
Bulrush	Scirpus sp.
Bupleurum	Bupleurum sp.
Burnet, salad or garden	Sanguisorba minor (Poterium sanguisorba)
Buttercup	Ranunculus sp.
Buxifolium	Leiophyllum buxifolium
Canary grass	Phalaris canariensis
Candytuft	Iberis umbellata
Carnation	Dianthus caryophyllus
Catmint	Nepeta
Chamomile	Chamaemelum nobile
Chervil	Anthriscus cerefolium
Chicory, wild	Cichorium intybus
Chincherinchee	Ornithogalum thyrsoides
Chinese lantern	Physalis alkekengi
Chive	Allium schoenoprasum
Clematis	Clematis sp.
Clubrush	Scirpus sp.
Cornflower	Centaurea cyanus
Cotton lavender	Santolina chamaecyparissus
Cow parsley	UK: Anthriscus sylvestis USA: Heracleum lanatum
Cowslip	Primula veris
Daffodil	Narcissus sp.

Common name	Latin name
Daisy	Bellis perennis
Daylily	Hemerocallis sp.
Elderflower	Sambucus nigra
Endive	Cichorium endivia
Eryngo	Eryngium sp.
Everlasting	Helichrysum bracteatum
Feverfew	Chrysanthemum parthenium
Forget-me-not	Myosotis sylvatica
Foxglove	Digitalis sp.
Frisée (endive)	Cichorium endivia
Garlic, ornamental	Allium sp.
Geranium	Pelargonium sp.
Gerbera	Gerbera jamesonii
Globe artichoke	Cynara scolymus
Golden rod	Solidago sp.
Grape hyacinth	Muscari sp.
Gypsophila	Gypsophila paniculata
Hare's tail grass	Lagurus ovatus
Heart's ease	Viola tricolor
Hellebore	Helleborus sp.
Holly	Ilex aquifolium
Honesty	Lunaria annua
Honeysuckle	Lonicera sp.
Hop	Humulus lupulus
Hyssop	Hyssopus officinalis
Immortelle	Helichrysum bracteatum Helipterum roseum Xeranthemum annuum
Ivy	Hedera sp.
Jasmine	Jasminum sp.
Jonquil	Narcissus jonquilla
Knapweed	Centaurea
Lady's mantle	Alchemilla mollis
Larkspur	Delphinium consolida
Laurel, common or English	Prunus laurocerasus
Laurustinus	Viburnum tinus
Lavender	Lavandula angustifolia
Lemon balm	Melissa officinalis
Lemon mint	Mentha x piperita citrata
Lemon verbena	Lippia citriodora

Common name	Latin name
Lilac	Syringa sp.
Lily	Lilium sp.
Lily-of-the-valley	Convallaria majalis
Lobelia	Lobelia erinus
Lotus	Nelumbo lucifera
Love-in-a-mist	Nigella damascena
Love-lies-bleeding	Amaranthus caudatus
Maidenhair fern	Adiantum capillus-veneris
Maple	Acer sp.
Marguerite	Chrysanthemum frutescens
Marigold, pot	Calendula officinalis
Marjoram	Origanum marjorana
Meadowsweet	Filipendula ulmaria
Medick	Medicago falcata
Melilot	Melilotus altissima
Mimosa	Acacia sp.
Mint	Mentha sp.
Mock orange	Philadelphus sp.
Montbretia	Montbretia sp (Crocosmia sp.)
Nasturtium	Tropaeolum majus
Nipplewort	Lapsana communis
Oak, English	Quercus robur
Oats	Avena sp.
Onion, ornamental	Allium sp.
Oregano	Origanum vulgare
Pansy	Viola sp.
Pearl everlasting	Anaphalis sp.
Pennyroyal	Mentha pulegium
Peony	Paeonia lactiflora
Persian buttercup	Ranunculus asiaticus
Peruvian lily	Alstroemeria sp.
Pincushion flower	Scabiosa stellata
Pink	Dianthus x allwoodii
Poppy	Papaver
Potentilla	Potentilla sp.
Primrose	Primula vulgaris
Pulmonaria	Pulmonaria sp.
Quaking grass	Briza maxima
Queen Anne's lace	UK: Didiscus caeruleus USA: Daucus carota
Rock rose	Cistus
Rose	Rosa sp.
Rosemary	Rosmarinus officinalis
Rue	Ruta graveolens

Common name	Latin name
Safflower	Carthamus tinctorius
Sage	Salvia officinalis
Sandflower	Ammobium sp.
Scabious	Scabiosa stellata
Sea holly	Eryngium oliverianum
Sea lavender	Limonium sp.
Scented geranium	Pelargonium sp.
September flower	Aster sp.
Shepherd's purse	Capsella bursa-pastoris
Silver dollar	Lunaria annua
Silverweed	Potentilla anserina
Snow-on-the-mountain	Euphorbia marginata
Snowball flower	Viburnum opulus
Southernwood	Artemisia abrotanum
Spiraea	Spiraea sp.
Sprengeri fern	Asparagus sprengeri
Spurge	Euphorbia sp.
Statice	Limonium sinuatum
Strawflower	Helichrysum bracteatum
Sumach	Rhus typhina
Summer cypress	Kochia scoparia
Sunray	Helipterum roseum (Acroclinium roseum)
Sweet pea	Lathyrus odoratus
Tansy	Tanacetum vulgare
Teasel	Dipsacus sativus (Dipsacus fullonum)
Thyme	Thymus sp.
Tulip	Tulipa sp.
Venus's hair	Adiantum capillus-veneris
Vetch	Vicia sativa
Violet, sweet	Viola odorata
Viola	Viola
Virginia creeper	Parthenocissus quinquefolia
Water dropwort	Oenanthe fistulosa
Wheat	Triticum aestivum
Wild carrot	Daucus sp.
Winged everlasting	Ammobium sp.
Winter savory	Satureja montana
Witch hazel	Hamamelis sp.
Wood avens	Geum sp.
Xeranthemum	Xeranthemum annuum
Yarrow	Achillea sp.

INDEX